Singing Cowboys and All That Jazz

SINGING COWBOYS
And All That Jazz

A Short History of Popular Music in Oklahoma

By
WILLIAM W. SAVAGE, JR.

Illustrated by
Rebecca Bateman

UNIVERSITY OF OKLAHOMA PRESS
NORMAN

By William W. Savage, Jr.

The Cherokee Strip Live Stock Association (Columbia, Missouri, 1973)
(Editor) *Cowboy Life: Reconstructing an American Myth* (Norman, 1975)
(Editor, with David Harry Miller) *The Character and Influence of the Indian Trade in Wisconsin,* by Frederick Jackson Turner (Norman, 1977)
(Editor) *Indian Life: Transforming an American Myth* (Norman, 1977)
(Editor, with Stephen I. Thompson) *The Frontier: Comparative Studies,* vol. 2 (Norman, 1979)
The Cowboy Hero: His Image in American History and Culture (Norman, 1979)
Singing Cowboys and All That Jazz: A Short History of Popular Music in Oklahoma (Norman, 1983)

WITHDRAWN
UTSA Libraries

Library of Congress Cataloging in Publication Data

Savage, William W.
  Singing cowboys and all that jazz.

  Includes bibliographical and discographical references and index.
  1. Music, Popular (Songs, etc.)—Oklahoma—History and criticism. I. Title.
ML3477.7.04S3   1983   780'.42'09766   82-17560

For the musicians.

Contents

Preface

HISTORIES of Oklahoma, especially those used as text-books in the public schools, do not often speak of the state's contributions to American popular culture. Their concerns lie more with the fine arts than with popular ones, perhaps to counterbalance the national image of Oklahoma as part of the Dust Bowl, a wasteland abandoned by emigrants heading for California, and thus a place devoid of agreed-upon measures of culture: symphony, opera, ballet, and whatnot. Emphasis on the fine arts is not misplaced, in view of the considerable creative efforts of Oklahomans who pursue those forms; but emphasis at the expense of the popular arts is a disservice to many other Oklahomans whose efforts have been just as creative and perhaps more influential in shaping the larger contours of American culture. I shall discuss popular music in the pages that follow—blues, jazz, ragtime, gospel, country and western, and other popular forms—to provide what is in my view a necessary supplement to the texts. I offer the book to students and teachers of Oklahoma history, to any who live and work in Oklahoma and wish to learn something of this one aspect of their cultural heritage, and to Oklahomans removed elsewhere who retain their senses of place and—not coincidentally—pride.

The history of popular music (and by "popular" I mean that which is shared in one way or another by large numbers of people) is neither easy to know nor simple to write. The sources of that history are scattered, if in fact they exist at all, and often they are mired in hopeless contradiction. Who performed where, when, and with whom? Few observers and almost no musicians took notes; and in the early decades of this century, when so much happened musically, journalists did not lavish upon popular music the attention characteristic of periodical writing in the years since World War II. As the history emerges now, largely in the form of autobiography, the scholar is reminded anew of the weaknesses of old men's memories. As much as the historian regrets the admission, there are many things that we simply may not know, at least not with any degree of certainty. The scholar seeking to describe and analyze the New York jazz scene in the 1930s faces these problems, and they could hardly be less formidable for the student of the Oklahoma jazz scene in the 1930s. After all, things were supposed to happen in New York, and people paid attention. As much—and in some cases, more—happened in Oklahoma, but significantly fewer people took notice.

Commentaries on relevant sources, including phonograph recordings, are placed at the ends of each chapter for the convenience of any who wish to pursue these matters. In most cases, the recordings cited are currently available through normal retail outlets, but the individual who hopes to build a representative library of Oklahoma music and musicians is well advised to exercise patience. Record catalogs change as frequently as the weather, or so it seems; and generally the issues of smaller, lesser-known labels enjoy a longer catalog life than those of the larger companies. Still, it should be possible for school libraries to build good collections, and certainly they should make the effort. I have yet to meet a student in an Oklahoma history class who was not impressed by the music, or a teacher who was not fascinated by the possibilities.

In all prefatory honesty, I must issue the obvious caution: this small book is intended to be nothing more than an introductory word on the subject. I have tried merely to provide a starting point, a convenient overview for the general reader. I have included as much information and as many sources as seemed necessary for an introduction; most assuredly I have not attempted a definitive treatment. Perhaps these few chapters will stimulate fresh and extensive investigations. I hope so; and so may any performers or composers who find their names missing from the index. I assure as many of them as there may be that I intended no slight.

Many individuals have contributed to the completion of this book. Those who merit special thanks are my colleague Sidney D. Brown, Department of History, University of Oklahoma, who shared books and records and whose vast knowledge of jazz in the 1930s and 1940s increased my appreciation of the subject; James H. Lazalier, Social Sciences Division, Oscar Rose Junior College, a friend who guided me through the labyrinthine history of rock music and listened patiently to what he must then have recognized as ill-formed ideas; Barney Kessel, who kindly consented to talk about jazz, Muskogee, Charlie Christian, philosophy, and countless other matters of mutual interest; former students Wayne H. Gossard, Jr., of Dallas, Texas, and Steve Mathis, of Venice, California, who found obscure recordings and research materials; Rebecca Bateman, of Joplin, Missouri, who prepared the illustrations for this volume and put me on the trail of the Ragtime Kid; Jean Ware, manager of the Record Bar, of Norman, Oklahoma, who searched catalogs, supervised countless special orders, nobly tolerated my many interruptions of business routine, and introduced me to the Cowboy Twinkies; Terry Ware, Jim Herbst, and Alan Munde of Norman, Oklahoma, veteran musicians (and superior ones, too) who took time to talk about their careers and their aspirations; my friend Zelbert L. Moore, of Philadelphia, Pennsylvania, a scholar of remarkable capacity, who, as he has done so often before, kept me supplied with clippings, notes, and bibliography that would otherwise have escaped my notice; Wayne McDaniel, 1980-81 president of the Oklahoma Country Music Association, who answered innumerable questions; Russell D. Buhite, chair of the Department of History, University of Oklahoma, who provided steadfast administrative support; and Arrell M. Gibson, Department of History, University of Oklahoma, mentor, friend, and colleague who years ago suggested what Oklahoma history could be and who saw to it that people cared.

To these and others—students past and present, and strangers who, having heard a bit of this read at some meeting, introduced themselves by saying, "That reminds me . . ."—I express my deep gratitude. They are blameless for mistakes that I may have gone on to make despite their careful guidance.

Thanks also to Martha Penisten, who typed the manuscript. She, is, quite simply, the best and the brightest.

WILLIAM W. SAVAGE, JR.

Norman, Oklahoma

Singing Cowboys and All That Jazz

But I am sick of all the din
That's made in praising Verdi . . . .
— Edward Robert Bulwer-Lytton

1. Culture For a Song:
Oklahoma's Musical Environment

MUSIC travels with the people who play it. That is an observation more germane to the nineteenth century than to the twentieth, when radio and television carry the same tunes everywhere and stores from coast to coast sell the same records and tapes, blurring regional distinctions in musical culture in all but the most isolated corners of the nation. In the nineteenth-century West, however, and on the frontier of which Oklahoma was a part, those who wished to have music made it themselves. They fashioned or acquired instruments, or they sang without accompaniment, for their own amusement or for the amusement of family, friends, and neighbors. They danced on Saturday and sang hymns on Sunday. They played and sang in that brief time between supper and bed during the week, that one waking hour reserved for something besides work or prayer. Children learned to sing or play instruments from adults, and adults taught the songs of their own childhoods, the songs they had acquired in other places. Music travels with people, and many different groups of people immigrated to the land that would become Oklahoma. Each group contributed something to the creation of a vigorous musical environment.

The Plains Indians were originally immigrants, but they had been in residence so long that the Europeans who found them could accept them as indigenous. These people had music for ceremonial and social purposes, songs and instruments to accompany dances that might have spiritual significance or that might be nothing more than an exhibition by a young men's dancing fraternity. Plains Indian instruments included drums, rattles, and rasps—all rhythm instruments—but most Plains Indian groups also had musicians who played the flageolet, a kind of flute, used principally by young men during courtship. But courting or celebrating, Indian musicians did not much impress the Europeans who heard them, at least not favorably. Later, Anglo-Americans listened reluctantly as well, describing the music—or rather condemning it—as cacophonous and of hellish origin. "To European ears," Oscar Brand has noted, "the Indian music sounded ridiculous and unsingable." Still, as we shall see, Indian music did have some influence on the development of American popular music. In addition, it seems likely that Indian music changed to some extent as a result of Indian contact with Anglo-Americans. The Plains Indian "Forty-nine" songs, popular among such groups as the Kiowas in Oklahoma today, may have originated as a form of Indian protest in the nineteenth century. According to some scholars, they developed to accompany all-night dances designed to deprive United States soldiers of sleep.

Later Indian immigrants—the Five Civilized Tribes removed to the West by the federal government, beginning in the 1830s—had music, too; but it was no more impressive to European and Anglo-American ears than Plains Indian music was. But the Five Civilized Tribes also had black slaves (which partly explains why whites had bestowed the title "civilized" upon them), and the slaves possessed a music of their own. This was more familiar

4

stuff, more closely akin to English melodic forms than was the Indian music, because blacks began reconstructing their music on eastern plantations where, cut off from their African heritage and enslaved in an alien land, they were subjected to white — and musically that meant English — influences.

The early shouts, field hollers, and work songs of black slaves would eventually coalesce in that form of rural black folk music known as the blues, but in the slave experience there was also a strong religious current, inasmuch as religion holds the promise of release from earthly toil and trouble; and religious interest manifested itself in spiritual (later to become gospel) music. Slaves in Indian Territory had spirituals as well as work songs, and some of their music attracted a great deal of attention after the Civil War. Freedom scarcely changed conditions of life for blacks, and after the war they were singing the same songs they had sung as slaves.

"Uncle" Wallis Willis and "Aunt" Minerva were blacks who had labored as slaves on Choctaw cotton plantations near the Red River. After the Civil War, at a Choctaw boarding school, a minister named Alexander Reid heard them singing a spiritual:

> *Swing low, sweet chariot,*
> *Coming for to carry me home.*
> *Swing low, sweet chariot,*
> *Coming for to carry me home.*
> *I looked over Jordan, and what did I see,*
> *Coming for to carry me home?*
> *A band of angels coming after me,*
> *Coming for to carry me home.*

Reid transcribed the song, together with another of their spirituals, entitled "Steal Away to Jesus," and sent the music to the Jubilee Singers, of Fisk University, in Nashville, Tennessee. Subsequently, the Jubilee Singers performed the songs on a tour of the United States and Europe, and the world received perhaps the first of Oklahoma's musical gifts. Many more would follow.

Cowboys passed through Oklahoma in large numbers after the Civil War because many of the great cattle trails north from Texas crossed the then Indian Territory to railroad shipping points in Missouri and Kansas. Cowboys were musical people, if not by inclination, then because their jobs required it. On the trail for months at a time, cowboys sang to entertain their companions, to relieve the tedium of their work, and to soothe the cattle and discourage their tendency to stampede at night. Musically, cowboy skills and repertoire probably increased under the more sedentary influences of ranch life. Whereas the harmonica was the instrument best suited to the rigors of life on the trail, the more fragile guitar and fiddle might find a home in the bunkhouse; and ranch dwellers had more opportunities to play and sing in purely social community situations. The cowboy contributed significantly to the kind of dance music that would become popular among rural white audiences in the second and third decades of the twentieth century.

Cowboy songs told stories, and an interest in storytelling was a prominent feature of Oklahoma's developing musical environment. Cowboy music continued a ballad tradition that extended back through time and space from the Appalachian South to the British Isles. It is still an important tradition on the Southern Plains. As folk-rock musician Michael Murphey has observed, "Story-telling is a very heavy-duty trip in the Southwest. I think most people who grow up here are used to having relatives who tell a lot of stories, and they're steeped in that tradition." Certainly Murphey's contemporary music suggests that tradition, as do the songs of John Denver, himself the son of Oklahoma parents and a product of the musical environment of Oklahoma and the Southwest; Tulsa-born folksinger Sam Hinton; and former Oklahoma college student Ed McCurdy. Woody Guthrie was a better—and better-known—balladeer than any who followed him from the region, but his influence on American music is so pervasive that it requires treatment in a separate chapter.

The ballad tradition was evidently strong among the various groups of white settlers who came to Oklahoma Territory after 1889, or so one might judge from the variety of materials surviving for the scrutiny of modern musicologists. Ethel and Chauncey Moore, for example, collected more than six hundred ballad "titles, melodies, and texts" for their compendium of 1964, *Ballads and Folk Songs of the Southwest.* Most of the music came from the British Isles by way of the mountain South, and the Moores were able to collect most of it in or around Tulsa.

In the territorial period, historian Angie Debo has noted, Oklahomans "sang everywhere they met, and they played every instrument that came to hand." The musical environment of Oklahoma was thus enhanced by the blending of a number of musical traditions from different parts of the country. Towns were social centers no less than economic ones, and they served to draw together diverse peoples from the surrounding country-side for weekend social functions ranging from picnics and dances to church services. Cultural uniformity was difficult to find in those early days. Each church congregation, for example, might have its vocal efforts sustained by a multiplicity of hymnals, each brought to Oklahoma by its owner from wherever home used to be.

Immigration to Oklahoma did not end with the land runs and lotteries of the 1890s, or with statehood in 1907; in fact, it continues today, albeit to little effect as it concerns the present musical environment of the state. The production of music by individuals, families, and communities is less important than it once was, and thus—except for what is done by the local high-school marching band or a barbershop quartet or a church choir—it has fallen into the hands of entrepreneurs and pro-fessionals. If cultural stasis (and thereby, cultural loss) is the result, that is nevertheless a relatively recent development. Im-

7

migration—and to some extent, emigration, in the 1930s and 1940s—helped to maintain the vitality of Oklahoma's musical environment from the 1890s to the 1950s, and to extend Oklahoma's influence elsewhere. To understand the how and why of it, we might prepare a preliminary "cultural map" and use it to chart musical migration. Consider the following:

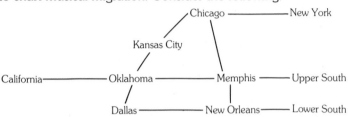

If we trace the evolution of American jazz, for example, we would trace migrations of blacks from the lower South westward from New Orleans to Texas, through Oklahoma, to Kansas City, and thence eastward again. Other routes exist, to be sure, but that is a major one. Similarly, the east-west axis from the upper South saw migrations of rural whites and blacks, some of whom had followed the Mississippi River from the delta region to Memphis. The Dallas-Kansas City axis was a principal artery for the movement of ragtime and jazz musicians. The New Orleans-Dallas-Oklahoma route brought admixtures of black folk music, white folk music, and Acadian (or "cajun") folk music. And so forth. The combinations, the interrelationships among regions and their peoples, are complex and have not yet been explored fully. The next chapters may amplify some of them, but the point here is this: Oklahoma was centrally located on the growing cultural map of the nation, and it functioned as a major musical crossroads for a moving and expanding population. The vigorous musical environment of Oklahoma was not an accidental thing. Some skeptics would say (and have said) that Oklahoma is the last place to look for meaningful cultural development; but any who know its history and understand something of the migrations of its people would say otherwise. On the map of the United States, beyond the population centers of the Northeast and the Far West, historical inquiry taps a muscular finger on the state of Oklahoma. Culturally, it is a likely spot—and perhaps the first place to look.

Sources

The introduction to Alan Lomax, *The Folk Songs of North America in the English Language* (Garden City, N.Y.: Doubleday & Co., 1960), offers a convenient discussion of cultural diversity and why people sang. Indian music is discussed in Robert H. Lowie, *Indians of the Plains* (Garden City, N.Y.: Natural History Press, 1963), and Alice Marriott and Carol K. Rachlin, *American Epic: The Story of the American Indian* (New York: New American Library, 1970). Travelers' accounts of Indian music are plentiful and offer many opportunities for comparison, for instance, Louis De Vorsey, Jr., ed., *De Brahm's Report of the General Survey in the Southern District of North America* (Columbia: University of South Carolina Press, 1971), for the late eighteenth century, and Richard Irving Dodge, *Our Wild Indians: Thirty-three Years' Personal Experience Among the Red Men of the Great West* (Hartford, Conn.: A. D. Worthington & Co., 1882), for the late nineteenth. Representative recordings of Plains Indian music in Oklahoma include *Kiowa Forty-Nine and Round Dance Songs* (Canyon C-6087) and *Kiowa Scalp and Victory Dance Songs* (Canyon C-6166). Of interest also are *Handgame of the Kiowa, Kiowa Apache & Comanche, Vols. 1 and 2* (Indian House IH 2501-2502). Doc Tate Nevaquaya, the noted Comanche painter, is responsible for something of a renaissance of Plains Indian flute music. An internationally known lecturer on Indian culture, Nevaquaya teaches young musicians to make as well as play this traditional instrument. The essential recording is *Comanche Flute Music* (Folkways 4328). The Oscar Brand quotation is from his *The Ballad Mongers: Rise of the Modern Folk Song* (n.p.: Minerva Press, 1967), p. 34.

There is a great debate over the derivation of black American folk music, and it grew in part from the heightening of ethnic consciousness in the 1960s that culminated in Afro-Americanism and finally in the "roots" syndrome of the 1970s. See, for example, the third chapter of Le Roi Jones, *Blues People: Negro Music in White America* (New York: William Morrow & Co., 1963), and the introduction to A. X. Nicholas, ed., *Woke Up This Mornin': Poetry of the Blues* (New York: Bantam Books, 1973). Because it is still fashionable to speak of black music as a political phenomenon rather than a cultural one, there is probably no sane treatment of the subject that would please everyone, but see Harold Courlander,

Negro Folk Music, U.S.A. (New York: Columbia University Press, 1963), and Marshall W. Stearns, *The Story of Jazz* (New York: New American Library, 1958), especially chaps. 8, 9, and 12. *See also* Frank Parman, *This Land, Your Land, My Land: A Brief Survey of Migration and Culture in Oklahoma* (Oklahoma City: Oklahoma Arts and Humanities Council, 1979), and W. E. B. DuBois, *The Souls of Black Folk* (Chicago: A. C. McClurg & Co., 1907), pp. 252-56. Useful background recordings are *African Journey: A Search for the Roots of the Blues* (Vanguard SRV-73014/5), which was produced and recorded by blues authority Samuel B. Charters; *Jazz, Volume 1: The South* (Folkways FJ 2801); and *The Story of the Blues* (Columbia G 30008).

The ballad tradition in cowboy music is demonstrated by *Authentic Cowboys and Their Western Folksongs* (RCA-LPV522) and Harry Jackson, *The Cowboy: His Songs, Ballads & Brag Talk* (Folkways FH 5723). See John A. Lomax, *Cowboy Songs and Other Frontier Ballads* (New York: Sturgis and Walton, 1910), and Ramon F. Adams, *The Old-Time Cowhand* (New York: Collier Books, 1971), chap. 5. The Murphey quotation is from Jan Reid, *The Improbable Rise of Redneck Rock* (Austin: Heidleberg Publishers, 1974), p. 249. Murphey's album *Geronimo's Cadillac* (A&M SP4358) offers examples of the ballad tradition in contemporary popular music and has some application to Oklahoma history. John Denver's Oklahoma antecedents are discussed in James M. Martin, *Rocky Mountain Wonder Boy: John Denver* (New York: Pinnacle Books, 1977). Other representative albums are *Sam Hinton Sings the Songs of Men* (Folkways FA 2400) and Ed McCurdy, *Ballad Singer's Choice* (Tradition 1003).

The ballad tradition and the migration of culture may be illustrated by a comparison of song titles and texts in the Moores' book (Norman: University of Oklahoma Press, 1964) with those in Arthur Kyle Davis, Jr., ed., *Traditional Ballads of Virginia* (Charlottesville: University Press of Virginia, 1969).

The Debo quotation is taken from her *Oklahoma: Foot-loose and Fancy-free* (Norman: University of Oklahoma Press, 1949), p. 212. Much about the state's early musical environment may be discerned from that volume and from Angie Debo, *Prairie City: The Story of an American Community* (New York: Alfred A. Knopf, 1944).

The complexity of American musical traditions and their diffusion is demonstrated by the almost overwhelming variety of recordings contained in the three-volume, six-disc *Anthology of American Folk Music* (Folkways FA 2951-2953), which must be heard to be believed. It is a basic item that no student of American music can ignore and that no library should be without.

2. Black Music, White Music,
One Music

OKLAHOMA is the birthplace of the blues as a notated, published musical form. It was five years after statehood, and a young violinist named Hart Wand managed the fortunes of a small dance band in Oklahoma City. Wand's father, a pharmacist, had immigrated to Oklahoma during the territorial period and had opened a drugstore in Oklahoma City in those first days when everyone lived and conducted business in tents. Things had changed by 1912. Wand worked for his father, and, when business was slow, he would retire to the back room of the drugstore to practice the violin. He was refining a tune he wanted to perform with his band, a simple melody that had come to him, one supposes, the way most music comes to most composers.

Wand's father had another employee, a Texan who swept the floors, moved merchandise, and served as general factotum. Something of a whistler, he used to accompany Hart Wand during those practice sessions. One day, listening to Wand's new tune, he remarked, "That gives me the blues to go back to Dallas."

Later, a pianist named Anabelle Robbins arranged the tune,

and Hart Wand published it in Oklahoma City under the title "Dallas Blues" in March, 1912, several months before the appearance of W. C. Handy's "Memphis Blues," often (but erroneously) celebrated as the first published blues song.

The first printing of "Dallas Blues" sold out within a week. There was a second printing and, by September, a third. It was an instrumental (somebody else added words a decade later) and, because it was simple to play, its popularity spread quickly. In a matter of weeks "Dallas Blues" could be heard up and down the Mississippi River, wherever music was played.

Hart Wand was a white man. The whistling Texan was black. The musical genre to which Wand contributed is universally identified as black.

Elliott Charles Adnopoz was born in Brooklyn, New York, in 1931; but years later, he claimed to have been born on a ranch in Oklahoma. Robert Allen Zimmerman was born in Duluth, Minnesota, in 1941; but years later he claimed to have been born in Oklahoma. When Adnopoz became a musician, he called himself Ramblin' Jack Elliott, but others called him the son of Woody Guthrie. When Zimmerman became a musician, he called himself Bob Dylan, but others called him the grandson of Woody Guthrie.

Adnopoz met Woody Guthrie in 1951, while young Zimmerman was learning to play the harmonica and guitar in Minnesota by listening to Hank Williams records and to a powerful Little Rock, Arkansas, radio station that aired bluesmen like Muddy Waters and Howlin' Wolf. Later, Zimmerman would listen to Ramblin' Jack Elliott's records, wherein Elliott imitated Woody Guthrie. Zimmerman thought he was listening to an Oklahoma cowboy.

In 1960, Robert Zimmerman read Woody Guthrie's *Bound for Glory*, a memoir published when Zimmerman was two years old. As Bob Dylan, he headed east to meet Guthrie, who was by then hospitalized in New Jersey with Huntington's chorea. In 1961, sitting in a New York club with some other musicians, Dylan learned that Jack Elliott was really Elliott Adnopoz, a middle-class Jew from Brooklyn. Dylan "fell off his chair," according to Dave Von Ronk. "He rolled under the table, laughing like a madman . . . . We had all suspected Bobby was Jewish, and that proved it." Dylan stayed under the table. Occasionally, someone would lean over and shout "Adnopoz!" And Robert Allen Zimmerman would begin laughing again.

Bob Dylan visited Woody Guthrie and became his disciple. Woody Guthrie had taught his son, Arlo, to play the harmonica at the age of three. When Arlo was thirteen, Bob Dylan showed him a new way to play it.

Woody Guthrie had learned to play the harmonica in Okemah, Oklahoma. A black teenager taught him how.

Bob Wills, the patriarch of western-swing music until his death in 1975, spent the best years of his musical career in Tulsa. Between 1934 and 1942, performing on radio station KVOO, Wills built a six-man string band into an eighteen-piece orchestra, the fabled Texas Playboys, known for its repertoire of dance music and its western "style."

Wills built his orchestra by adding reeds, brass, and percussion to his string section. Without the strings—guitars, fiddles, banjo, and whatnot—he would have had a jazz band. Many of his musicians began as jazz performers, and, as it was, Wills borrowed heavily from jazz repertoire. He played a great deal of blues music as well.

Bob Wills had learned black music while growing up in Texas. He lived and worked among blacks. He learned the music directly from black musicians, not from records or radio.

Once, an inebriated Bob Wills hired a black trumpet player

in Tulsa. The black Texas Playboy survived for one performance. A sober Bob Wills decided that Oklahomans were un-
prepared to accept a black man playing black music in a white
orchestra.

What color is music? To this point, I have written of black
music, white music, Indian music, and so forth, but without defining the terms. I should like to enjoy the comforts of scholarly
dogmatism, but there appear to be no simple definitions. If
music has hues, they are the ones of the people who play it,
or so we may theorize. Black music, accordingly, would be any
music composed or performed by blacks. White music would
be that which is composed or performed by whites. But what
if whites perform music composed by blacks? Does the music
bear the label of its origin? There is, of course, the matter of
style, and discussions of style go something like this: It does
not matter *what* music is played. The important consideration
is *how* it is played. Thus, white music performed by blacks is
black, because black performances differ significantly from white
performances. The notes may be the same, but the inflection
is different.

But style may be copied—and copied so effectively that an
Adnopoz from Brooklyn or a Zimmerman from Duluth can be
accepted by audiences as the genuine article from Oklahoma.
Or, to carry the argument full circle, are we to accept the
labels of ethnicity and conclude that Ramblin' Jack Elliott and
Bob Dylan compose and perform Jewish music?

If arguments over style and ethnicity are counterproductive,
it is because music—no less than the larger American culture
of which it is a part—defies segregation. No cultural arbiter says
to the musician, "You cannot perform that music. It is identified
with an ethnic group to which you do not belong." Or, "You
cannot play the saxophone in that style. If you do, people may
take you for something other than what you are." In a vigorous

14

environment culture does not condemn the individual to a lifetime with his antecedents if other traditions or modes of expression seem more satisfying.

Pop psychology preaches that people who abandon their backgrounds are likely to become neurotic, but history offers little supporting evidence. Cultural stagnation derives more from unwavering ancestor worship than from the gradual cultural changes that are part of the historical process. Immigrants lose the accents and mannerisms of one region as they acquire the corresponding characteristics of another—unless they consciously resist, at which point they become culturally dysfunctional in the context of their spatial and temporal environment.

But in Oklahoma, one does not long contemplate the abandonment of heritage, owing to the presence of so much that is new. Hart Wand wrote the music of his environment, a music influenced by the passage of diverse groups through a burgeoning territory and a new state. Bob Wills and Woody Guthrie absorbed the music of their childhoods and adapted it to express the perceptions of their adult years. They were all, therefore, culturally honest men. It is of interest that their music encouraged imitation, even if the fact of imitation suggests that elsewhere in the nation there were cultural levels where vacuums existed, waiting to be filled by that which Oklahoma had ready for export.

I have described Oklahoma as a musical crossroads and spoken of its vigorous musical environment. It was, as well, a musical melting pot (in the mixed metaphor of cultural description), a place for the blending of different musical traditions. Black musicians and white musicians borrowed freely from each other, exchanging repertoires and musical ideas and adopting new styles. The result was remarkable cultural growth. Color seemed not to matter to musicians (although, as Wills learned, it did to audiences) because they were interested primarily in the music and not who played it. In that regard, the cultural environment occupied a plane far in advance of the social environment. If blacks and whites in Oklahoma in the first half of the twentieth century could not publicly mingle as performers or as listeners, then they did so privately. The exchange went on, despite rigid social strictures. In the 1930s the Texas Playboys belted out "St. Louis Blues," "Empty Bed Blues," "Basin Street Blues," "Wang Wang Blues," and "Mean Mamma Blues" for white audiences, while black Oklahoma fiddler Claude Williams dished up white country traditions with Andy Kirk's Clouds of Joy for black audiences, and Woody Guthrie played blues and sang cowboy songs to nearly everyone. And if that were not enough, Jack Teagarden, the blackest white jazzman who ever lived, was off performing with Paul Whiteman, using what he had learned as a boy trying to imitate the sounds of an Indian powwow on his trombone over at the Oklahoma City fairgrounds. A melting pot, indeed.

All of this argues strongly that segregated audiences were listening to much the same music performed by segregated musicians, and that, if you blindfolded everyone, nobody would know the difference, either by style or repertoire.[1] If that is so, and the distinctions between musical forms are derived from visual rather than auditory data, from the pigmentation of the musician rather than the sounds from his instrument, then the distinctions are superficial ones and deserve considerably less attention than they customarily receive. The ethnic identification of musicians may be important to the delineation of the cultural environment in its relationship to the geographical setting and the social environment, and so I shall continue the

---

[1] Legendary stories are told about just that sort of thing. Listening to a recording by black tenor saxophonist Buddy Collette and asked to identify the performer, Miles Davis said, "All those white tenor players sound alike to me." Listening to the all-black Billy Taylor quartet, Roy Eldridge remarked, "They could be Eskimos for all I know." One could accuse neither of those distinguished black trumpet players of having untutored ears.

16

practice whenever it seems appropriate; but labels are convenient to the language and should not be interpreted to suggest cultural segregation, for there seems to have been little of that in Oklahoma's musical history. If there was not the "one music" suggested by the title of this chapter, neither were there several radically different or widely separated ones. An understanding of that fact is essential to the comprehension of what happened in Oklahoma and what made its musical legacy so notable.

Sources

Tony Russell, *Blacks, Whites and Blues* (New York: Stein and Day, 1970), and Nick Tosches, *Country: The Biggest Music in America* (New York: Stein and Day, 1977), concern musical exchanges between blacks and whites. Samuel B. Charters, *The Country Blues*, rev. ed. (New York: Da Capo Press, 1975), recounts the story of Hart Wand, while Anthony Scaduto, *Bob Dylan* (New York: New American Library, 1973), discusses the interrelationships between Guthrie, Adnopoz, and Zimmerman. Scaduto's book is the source of the Von Ronk quotation. Bob Wills's biographer is Charles Townsend, whose "Bob Wills and Western Swing: The Oklahoma Years, 1934-1942," in *Rural Oklahoma*, ed. Donald E. Green (Oklahoma City: Oklahoma Historical Society, 1977), pp. 84-100, is a convenient distillation of relevant material from his larger work, *San Antonio Rose: The Life and Music of Bob Wills* (Urbana: University of Illinois Press, 1976). Jack Teagarden's Oklahoma boyhood is discussed in Bill Burchardt, "Fantabulous Teagardens," *Oklahoma Today*, Fall 1961, pp. 4-5, 30-31, and in Leonard F. Guttridge's pamphlet accompanying Time Life Records' *Jack Teagarden* (STL-J08) in the *Giants of Jazz* series. Teagarden said (p. 10), "And when they would sing those Indian chants, you know, that came natural to me too. I could play an Indian thing—just pick up my horn and play it to where you couldn't tell the difference. I don't know how that came so natural."

17

3. Oklahoma City and the Blue Devils

BENNIE Moten was a busy man, and his Kansas City, the Kansas City of the 1920s, was a busy place. Bennie Moten had a band, and he made money playing jazz.

Busy men do not enjoy having problems, but Bennie Moten had a big one in 1929. There were people he had to avoid, people who played better jazz than the musicians in his band, people who had thrashed his men in a battle of bands, a "carving contest" at Paseo Hall—his own backyard—in 1928. Moten's pride was hurt, but beyond that he had his reputation to consider. Bennie Moten had boasted of having the best band in the southwest and perhaps in the entire country. He could not abide the notion that there were better musicians elsewhere. He did not like the competition.

There were people Bennie Moten had to avoid. He could not risk another costly encounter. He could not afford another meeting with the Oklahoma City Blue Devils.

The two major periods of black immigration to Oklahoma were 1890-1910, when the state's black population reached 137,000, and the years immediately after World War I, the boomtown era of the petroleum industry. Characteristic of the

18

first period was the establishment of a number of all-black communities in Oklahoma, including Langston (1891), Clearview (1903), and Boley (1904). These towns developed marching bands, cornet bands, and concert bands, just as other territorial communities had. Yet, in these black towns social pressures were at work to curb musical expression, lest it induce idleness—or worse—and damage the image of blacks that townsmen hoped to offer the outside world. There was among the God-fearing, moreover, a perceived difference between secular music and religious music; and secular music received careful scrutiny as a potentially bad influence. These attitudes were also present among blacks in towns with biracial populations, as we shall see, but they were less influential than in the more burdensome social environments of the black towns.

The culturally permissive biracial communities—and this permissiveness, one must recall, is measured by only slight degrees—allowed the flowering of popular music in Oklahoma in the territorial period. In the 1890s, for example, El Reno was a center for ragtime musicians, and composers and performers like Scott Joplin and Otis Saunders were frequent visitors. S. Brunson Campbell, a sixteen-year-old piano player known professionally as the "Ragtime Kid," worked in El Reno in 1900 and recalled it as a wide-open town, "a beehive of gamblers."

The revival of national interest in ragtime music—and particularly in Scott Joplin's music—sparked by Marvin Hamlisch's score for George Roy Hill's Oscar-winning film, *The Sting* (1973), did not bring much awareness of the ragtime milieu, which consisted of saloons, parlors in houses of ill repute, and other low haunts. Otis Saunders, for example, played piano in Scar Face Mary's Oklahoma City brothel in 1898 and returned to the job in 1907 after a stint in Guthrie. Bawdy-house parlors were certainly another arena for cultural exchanges between blacks and whites—and another argument against secular music in black communities—but ragtime music could be

S. Brunson Campbell

heard in more respectable places as well. S. Brunson Campbell played Joplin's "Maple Leaf Rag" for Pawnee Bill at El Reno's Kerfoot Hotel in 1900, a memorable experience for both men. When they met in Tulsa twenty years later, Pawnee Bill asked the Ragtime Kid to play it again.

Ragtime musicians often left Oklahoma because more money waited elsewhere. Chicago especially attracted them, for in addition to the money, Chicago offered a more tolerant racial climate. But many other musicians remained in Oklahoma, and ragtime was not the only music in the territory.

It is a cultural commonplace to speak of New Orleans as the cradle of American jazz, since it was the home of Bunk Johnson, King Oliver, and Louis Armstrong, to name but three of the legendary musicians who performed there, and since its contemporary image is so involved with evocations of its musical past. But as we have seen, music moves with people, and not everyone with musical ability immigrated to New Orleans. The brass marching bands—the Eureka, the Excelsior, the Onward Brass Band, and others—that helped New Orleans make cultural history at the turn of the century (the jazz funeral, Rampart Street, and Storyville became part of the American idiom) were merely the best known. But the best band of all may have marched in the streets of Oklahoma City, under the leadership of Andrew Rushing (trumpet), Millidge Winslett (trombone), George Sparks (peck horn), and Jim Bronson (clarinet). Groups like this added much to Oklahoma's musical heritage and built appreciative audiences for musicians yet to come.

The black migrations westward after World War I increased those audiences, and, until the Depression's grip tightened on the state, Oklahomans could hear some of the best jazz musicians in the world. They did not perform with bands that blew in from the coast for a one-night stand. They performed with groups resident in Tulsa and Oklahoma City.

Walter Page and Coleman Lewis organized the Oklahoma

City Blue Devils in 1923 or 1924. Lewis subsequently gave up music for a political career, and Page became leader of the group. According to Page, the original Blue Devils consisted of Oran ("Hot Lips") Page (no relation to Walter), James Simpson, and Jimmy Lu Grand on trumpet; Dan Minor and Eddie Durham on trombone; Reuben Roddy, Ted Manning, and Buster Smith on reeds; Turk Thomas on piano; Reuben Lynch on guitar; Alvin Burroughs on drums; and Walter Page on string bass, tuba, and baritone saxophone. Subsequent changes in personnel added trombonist Emir ("Bucket") Coleman, trumpet player Harry Youngblood, pianist Willie Lewis, and drummer Edward ("Crackshot") McNeil.

The Oklahoma City Blue Devils was a commonwealth band, or one in which important questions—who should be hired? what fees should the band charge? where should the band perform?—were settled by the vote of the majority; and its receipts, after expenses, were divided equally among the members. The band operated from Oklahoma City's Ritz Ballroom, playing dates in Shawnee, Chickasha, Tulsa, Enid, El Reno, and elsewhere around the state. The Blue Devils played the Ritz each winter and the Dreamland Ballroom in Little Rock, Arkansas, each summer, touring throughout Oklahoma, Nebraska, Kansas, Missouri, Arkansas, and Texas in the fall and spring. Occasionally, tours carried the musicians as far west as Colorado and New Mexico and as far north as Iowa and Minnesota. They traveled by car, the make and number of vehicles depending upon the group's income in any particular year, and they lived in segregated rooming houses or hotels, although sometimes in smaller towns they stayed in private homes. They made enough money—at least before 1929—to live comfortably.

Jazz bands in the Southwest frequently engaged each other in musical "battles," in which one group would try to surpass its opponent in volume, style, and repertoire. A visiting band would play opposite a local band in its own ballroom, and the bandleaders would actively promote the contests. They might plaster a town with handbills or advertise in local newspapers, but each would claim that his musicians were the best in the region, and each would forecast the swift and sure defeat of the competing group.

The Blue Devils excelled in such battles, so much so, in fact, that other bands were reluctant to face the Oklahoma group. And if other bands feared the original Blue Devils, they had even more reason to avoid the band as new performers were recruited. These included Lester Young (tenor saxophone), Jimmy Rushing (vocalist), and, from the East, a piano player named William Basie. They made the Oklahoma City Blue Devils the best collection of musicians in the Southwest and one of the best in the United States.

Lester Young was born in 1909 in Woodville, Mississippi, the son of a Tuskegee alumnus who taught him to play the violin, trumpet, saxophone, and drums. He grew up in New Orleans, and by the age of ten he was playing drums in the Young family band. In 1922 he turned finally to the saxophone and traveled with his father, who worked the carnival circuit in the Northern Plains as part of a minstrel show. Lester Young became a jazz musician in the late 1920s, earned many honors during his career, and was, by the time of his death in 1959, the foremost jazz saxophonist.

Jimmy Rushing was a particularly valuable recruit for the Blue Devils. Born in Oklahoma City in 1903, he grew up in a musical family: his mother and brother were singers, and his father was bandsman Andrew Rushing. He learned to play the piano and the violin by ear, and he studied music at Douglass High School. He was the pianist at high school dances, then known as "drags." Rushing spent time in Tulsa and recalled hearing a good blues singer (known only as "Cut") there as early as 1918. Cut's band contained tenor and alto saxophones,

Lester Young

a trumpet, a sousaphone, and drums, and Rushing would later note that the musicians were "not from New Orleans. Most of them were born right around Tulsa." There were several other bands in the area, including two led by Ernie Fields. Rushing went on to Los Angeles and sang there briefly in the mid-1920s. He returned to Oklahoma with some valuable experience.

Rushing was singing in his father's lunchroom when the Blue Devils discovered him—singing and cooking and pouring root beer. He was short and fat—he would become known as "Mr. Five-by-Five"—and sang with tremendous volume. He had to. There were no microphones for singers until around 1933, and unless a vocalist could match or exceed the volume of trumpets and trombones, he could not be heard in those crowded dance halls, and thus he would be superfluous and soon unemployed. Megaphones provided some help, but even so, said Rushing, "You had to have a good pair of lungs—strong!" He did. His voice, Ross Russell has remarked, was like another instrument, and even when the Blue Devils played their loudest, that voice could not be drowned out.

That was Bennie Moten's problem—drowning out the Blue Devils—and he had to do something about it.

Moten reportedly tried to acquire the Blue Devils wholesale, offering Walter Page continued leadership of the band but proposing to attach the Moten name to it. Page refused, and Moten, fearing the consequences, began raiding the Blue Devils; that is, he made offers to individual musicians to join his band. Bennie Moten wanted the best, and eventually he got them. Jimmy Rushing, Bill Basie, and Eddie Durham left the Blue Devils in 1929, Oran Page departed in 1930, and, in 1932, Walter Page left as well. Moten offered the security of hard cash—his Kansas City, with its corrupt, boss-ridden government and its hyperactive nightlife hardly noticed the Depression—

Jimmy Rushing

and record contracts. The Blue Devils, the best in the Southwest, had managed to record only two songs during their tenure in Oklahoma City.

Buster Smith took over leadership of the Blue Devils after Walter Page went to Kansas City. Other musicians joined the band briefly—saxophonist Ben Webster, who had begun his professional career as a pianist in Enid, was one of them—but the Depression was in full swing by then, and times were hard for jazzmen in the Southwest. Ballrooms and clubs where the Blue Devils had played before had either closed their doors or were about to, and that a commonwealth band could manage to stay together at all under those circumstances is something of a miracle. As it was, the Blue Devils lasted only a while longer. Smith took the band to the East in search of better times, but none were to be found in Virginia or West Virginia, and the Blue Devils, as Smith recalled, "hoboed all the way to St. Louis." Bennie Moten found the musicians there late in 1933 and hired those who had no other plans, including Smith, Lester Young, Jap Jones, and Theodore Ross.

So Bennie Moten had the Oklahoma City Blue Devils intact after all, and his fears of "carving contests" could be allowed to subside. But Moten had little time left to enjoy his success. He died in 1935 during a tonsillectomy, and his brother, Bus Moten, took over the band. Bus held it together for six short months.

Bill Basie took some of the old Blue Devils and organized a new band. In time, with this nucleus, Bill Basie, the piano player from Red Bank, New Jersey—the young man Jimmy Rushing had heard playing on a Tulsa sidewalk as a ballyhoo artist and front man for "Gonzel White and the Big Jamboree" and had recruited for the Blue Devils—built the musical aggregation that would revolutionize American jazz: the Count Basie Orchestra. And if you listen to Basie's recordings made in the

27

late 1930s, you will hear them: Dan Minor, Eddie Durham, Lester Young, Jimmy Rushing, and Walter Page—the old Oklahoma City Blue Devils.

Oran Page went on to form his own band. Reuben Roddy moved to New Orleans to march with the Eureka. Buster Smith stayed in Kansas City and performed with various groups, but later he joined the Basie orchestra as an arranger, after Basie had taken his musicians to New York City.

Jimmy Rushing, who died in 1972, enjoyed his greatest success and acquired his considerable reputation as Basie's vocalist between 1935 and 1950. Apart from the Blue Devils alumni, however, other Oklahomans had ties to Basie's band. Big Ed Lewis, born in Eagle City in 1909, spent ten years in Basie's trumpet section. A veteran of Moten's group, he joined Basie in 1937 and, according to Preston Love, played lead trumpet on almost all of the classic Basie recordings of the late 1930s. Love claimed that Lewis was responsible for much of the Basie "sound," and that he was probably the most overlooked of the original Basie musicians. His contemporaries called his playing "funky," and Love contended that his dedication to the band contributed significantly to its rise in popularity. "He may even have burned his lip out by playing *all* the lead in the young powerhouse band of 1937, 1938, and early 1939."

And Marshall Royal from Sapulpa, who had doubled on clarinet and alto saxophone for Les Hite, Lionel Hampton, and others, and had occasionally sided for Louis Armstrong, helped Basie organize a new band in 1951—a move that economic circumstances dictated as the big-band era closed. In the 1950s, Royal served as Basie's musical director, leading the band on most occasions while the Count attended to the keyboard. Another member of that group was Frank Wess, who joined Basie in 1953. Born in Kansas City, Missouri, Wess had spent the summers of his childhood studying saxophone at Langston University; in 1932, at age 10, he had met Don Byas

Count Basie

there. Byas, a saxophonist from Muskogee, performed with Basie in the 1940s.

Oklahoma was the matrix from whence came much of the best of American jazz. Without the Blue Devils the history of jazz would be quite a different thing; and when we read drummer Jo Jones's statement, "The greatest band I've heard was Mr. Walter Page's Blue Devils," we would do well to remember.

The 1920s and 1930s were surely the golden years of jazz in Oklahoma, or so they must seem from the untroubled perspective of the brightly packaged vinyl discs that now recall them to at least one of our senses. It is easy enough to forget, listening to Basie and Rushing, the agricultural depression that wracked Oklahoma in advance of the other one, the capital-d Depression that coincidentally ushered in alternate periods of drought and flood and dust. It is easy to forget, too, the Tulsa race riot, the violent deaths, the sad times when a university administrator wore the bed sheet of the Ku Klux Klan and governors abused the power of their office. That four-four beat drives it all away.

And it is easy to imagine that the music was everyone's medicine, a specific for the ills brought on by the few who were not listening, or to see it binding together communities by marking common goals. We may flip a switch, adjust the volume, and close our eyes to visit Halley Richardson's Oklahoma City shoeshine parlor and listen with Ralph Ellison as he "first heard Lester Young jamming in a shine chair, his head thrown back, his horn even then outthrust, his feet working on the footrests."

But reality plays a harsher note, and reality sits in the first chair. Those were bad times if you were white. If you were black, they were worse, because you had more than social, economic, and political problems to overcome. You had cultural problems, too, and they had to do with your ability to be yourself. Those community pressures were at work, the out-growth of Booker T. Washington's notions of how blacks should behave to gain the acceptance of whites. If you were a kid, your mother did not want you to listen to the kind of music the Blue Devils made. It was not decent. It was not respectable.

Institutions often intensified community pressures. In the year that Walter Page and Coleman Lewis organized the Blue Devils, Langston University's music curriculum emphasized the works of Schumann, Mendelsohn, and Rubinstein. In the 1950s, when Marshall Royal and the Basie band were swinging, Langston's music students were forbidden to form off-campus bands with-out faculty approval, nor could the students perform any music on the campus or away from it without faculty approval.

And in the 1950s, Ralph Ellison recalled the reaction of his Oklahoma City public-school teachers thirty years before to blues and jazz—and even spirituals. They would, he wrote, "have destroyed them and scattered the pieces."

Perhaps white kids who wanted to hear "Turkey in the Straw" had the same problems. But it is unlikely that they did.

Sources

The best introduction to the history of black people in the state is Jimmie Lewis Franklin, *The Blacks in Oklahoma* (Norman: University of Okla-homa Press, 1980). See also William Loren Katz, *The Black West*, rev. ed. (Garden City, N.Y.: Anchor Press/Doubleday, 1973), chap. 9. Com-munity attitudes are treated in Norman L. Crockett, *The Black Towns* (Lawrence: Regents of Press of Kansas, 1979).

S. Brunson Campbell's recollections are contained in Rudi Blesh and Harriet Janis, *They All Played Ragtime* (New York: Oak Publications, 1971); in James Haskins, with Kathleen Benson, *Scott Joplin* (New York: Stein and Day, 1980); and in *Musigram* 1, no. 11 (February 1964): 105-12. Splendid examples of the ragtime genre may be heard performed by Joshua Rifkin on the three-volume *Piano Rags by Scott Joplin* (None-such H-71248, H-71264, H-71305).

Biographies of many of the musicians mentioned in this chapter and in chapters 5 and 8 are contained in Leonard Feather, *The New Edition* of the Encyclopedia of Jazz (New York: Horizon Press, 1960), and John Chilton, *Who's Who of Jazz: Storyville to Swing Street* (Philadelphia: Chilton Book Company, 1972).

Ross Russell, *Jazz Style in Kansas City and the Southwest* (Berkeley: University of California Press, 1971), chapter 9, contains Buster Smith's account of the Oklahoma City Blue Devils. Also useful are Franklin S. Driggs, "Kansas City and the Southwest," in Nat Hentoff and Albert J. McCarthy, eds., *Jazz* (New York: Grove Press, 1961), pp. 189-230, and Hannah D. Atkins, "The Jazzmen," *Oklahoma Today,* Winter 1969-70, pp. 14-18. Albert Murray, *Stomping the Blues* (New York: McGraw-Hill Book Co., 1976), discusses the Blue Devils and charts the evolution of Basie's music. Jimmy Rushing's recollections, Preston Love's comments on Ed Lewis, and the Jo Jones quotation appear in Stanley Dance, *The World of Count Basie* (New York: Charles Scribner's Sons, 1980), pp. 18-19, 53, 157-58; for an interview with Marshall Royal, see pp. 164-74, and for Frank Wess's background, see p. 186. See also John Hammond, with Irving Townsend, *John Hammond on Record: An Autobiography* (New York: Ridge Press, 1977), chap. 18.

The Blue Devils' two recordings, "Blue Devil Blues" and "Squabblin'," may be heard on *Territory Bands, 1926-31* (Historical HLP-26). Lester Young's first recordings, made with Basie and Walter Page, are included on *The Lester Young Story, Volume 1* (Columbia CG 33502). Young's *Pres: The Complete Savoy Recordings* (Savoy 2202), with Basie and Ed Lewis, is also of interest. A Basie library would include *The Best of Count Basie* (MCA 2-4050), *Good Morning Blues* (MCA 2-4108), *Blues by Basie* (Columbia PC 36824), and *Super Chief* (Columbia CG 31224), all of which contain Jimmy Rushing vocals and feature former Blue Devils or Oklahoma-born musicians, for instance, Lewis, Dan Minor, Young, Walter Page, Eddie Durham, Claude Williams, Don Byas. Rushing's *Mister Five by Five* (Columbia C2 36419) is a showcase for his talents. Results of Basie's collaboration with Marshall Royal are contained on *Count Basie: Sixteen Men Swinging* (Verve VE-2-2517). Royal's recent work may be heard on *Royal Blue* (Concord CJ-125).

Ralph Ellison's memories of the Oklahoma City jazz scene in the era of the Blue Devils are found in his *Shadow and Act* (New York: Random House, 1964), pp. 187-98. For his discussion of Jimmy Rushing, see pp. 241-46. Sheldon Harris, *Blues Who's Who: A Biographical Dictionary of Blues Singers* (New Rochelle, N.Y.: Arlington House, 1979), pp. 445-48, offers the best chronology of Rushing's career. The music program at Langston is described in Zella J. Black Patterson, *Langston University: A History* (Norman: University of Oklahoma Press, 1979).

Oklahoma musicians prepared revivals of 1920s and 1930s jazz and the big-band era in 1980 and 1981. John B. Williams directed the Southwestern Historical Jazz Band in a Southwestern jazz concert in Norman in November, 1981, that featured the Blue Devils' "Squabblin'" and music by Bennie Moten, Basie, Alphonso Trent, Andy Kirk, and others.

And Count Basie played concerts in Oklahoma in February and March, 1982. Governor George Nigh signed a proclamation making Basie an "honorary native son of Oklahoma," albeit belatedly. Basie identified the Blue Devils as "the happiest band I've ever been in." See Juanita Freeman, "Basie Performance Ends 47-Year Career," *The Northeastern* (Tahlequah), March 3, 1982, pp. 1, 3.

4. The First Singing Cowboy

H E was Otto Gray, born near Ponca (a Santa Fe station on the Ponca Indian reservation, adjacent to present-day Ponca City) in the Indian Territory, about 1890. Before commercial recordings of cowboy singers were available, and before the singing cowboy became a fixture in motion pictures—before Gene or Roy or anyone else—Otto Gray was performing southwestern music for large audiences and establishing his reputation as the first singing cowboy in American show business.

William McGinty, of Stillwater, launched Gray's career in 1924 when he organized a "cowboy band" and hired Gray to manage it. McGinty was an old soldier, a veteran of the Spanish-American War, mustered out of Troop K, First United States Volunteer Cavalry, at the end of the campaign. That made him a "Rough Rider" and left him imbued with a strong sense of frontier tradition, perhaps derived in part from the fighting-cowboy notions of his former commanding officer, Theodore Roosevelt. In any case, McGinty's idea in forming the band was to preserve the music of the Old West and present it to a new generation of listeners.

Otto Gray and his Oklahoma Cowboys began performing over

Bristow radio station KFRU. The six-man string band (sometimes augmented by Mrs. Gray, known to history only as "Mom-
mie") gained good public acceptance with a repertoire that
included western standards like "The Cowboy's Lament" and
such forgettable tunes as "Who Broke the Lock on the Hen-
house Door?" Gray was a good musician and a better promoter
and the Oklahoma Cowboys were very quickly in the money.

Gray had a genuine product to sell. As it happened, his musicians were real cowboys, recruited for the band from different
Oklahoma ranches. Moreover, they were all competent musicians, capable of a polished professional performance, and that
sort of thing was in demand nationally. It was a time of widespread interest in cowboys, interest fueled by everything from
Saturday Evening Post serials to silent films and nurtured by
nostalgia for the wide-open spaces and the good-old-days of
pre-World War I America. Gray advertised in national show-
business publications like *Billboard* and successfully steered the
Oklahoma Cowboys to a series of lucrative jobs. Between 1928
and 1932, for example, Gray and the band traveled across the
country performing on radio and on vaudeville circuits. Booking
agencies in Chicago and New York coordinated vaudeville appearances, and an advance man traveled ahead of the band to
organize local publicity. Radio performances drummed up business for the stage shows, and personal appearances stimulated
interest in the radio performances. The band developed a following in some unexpected places: they were a hit, for example,
on the RKO vaudeville circuit in the northeastern states. They
appeared also on the Publix, Loew, and Fox circuits, and they
made money all the while.

The Oklahoma Cowboys traveled in a style indicative of their
prosperity. They owned three custom-built automobiles and two
custom trailers, moving across the landscape in a caravan sufficiently interesting for display on the group's Christmas cards.
Gray's limousine resembled a piece of railroad equipment, sport-

ing a cowcatcher on the front bumper and—believe it or not—an observation platform at the rear. The hood of another car carried a locomotive headlight and a small bell. Gray's auto reportedly cost $20,000 and contained considerable electronic equipment, including facilities for radio transmission. The vehicles were evidently as much of an attraction as the band itself.

The Oklahoma Cowboys performed from 1924 until 1936, disbanded, and faded into obscurity, perhaps because they made no recordings. Some members of the group went on to successful careers as country musicians, including Zeke Clements, a comic who became a crooner in the Eddy Arnold mold, and Whitey Ford, better known as the "Duke of Paducah," a comedian performing with Gene Autry and later a Grand Ole Opry regular. But Otto Gray has been virtually forgotten.

Zeke Clements once observed that Otto Gray had always been twenty years ahead of his time. He may have been, to be sure, the first singing cowboy, but he was also an important figure in the history of country music because he demonstrated the potential and the appeal of southwestern string bands. He applied the techniques of big-time show business to the promotion of what had been before 1924 merely rural dance music. Accordingly, Otto Gray stands as a precursor—and a notable one—of western swing. By the time the Oklahoma Cowboys disbanded, Bob Wills had already taken a page from Gray's book and moved to Tulsa to organize the Texas Playboys and complete the creation that some would call "Okie jazz." And Bob Wills would not be forgotten.

Otto Gray took an important first step in the commercialization and thereby the dissemination of rural white tradition. Bob Wills effectively completed that process, but laced his offerings with liberal quantities of black music, as we have seen. Wills gave western swing the form and format by which it is known today, and he prepared it for the changes that would come to the American music industry after World War II. If Gray had

Bob Wills

suggested the popularity of southwestern string-band music, Wills confirmed the public's affinity for it.

Tulsa radio station KVOO provided a 50,000-watt forum for Bob Wills's musical ideas. Wills developed a noontime show that grew to be one of the most popular hours on radio in the Southwest. At different periods, he and the Texas Playboys aired their music early in the morning, in the late afternoon, and late at night. There were live broadcasts from dances, and the Wills group played for many dances. As musicologist Guy Logsdon has noted, the history of Oklahoma's radio stations has yet to be written, and so we know but few of the details of Wills's — or anybody else's — daily schedules. From the assortment of materials available, however, we can learn something of the band's activities during the apex of Wills's popularity, reached, curiously enough, in his last year in Tulsa.

In April, 1942, Wills and the Playboys performed at dances in McAlester; Fort Smith (2); Ada; Oklahoma City (4); Coffeyville, Kansas; Fairview; Muskogee; Miami; Okemah; Seminole; Enid; and Pittsburg, Kansas. That adds up to sixteen dances. During the same month the band played ten dances at Cain's Academy in Tulsa. That adds up to twenty-six dance dates in a thirty-day period. All the dates were broadcast over KVOO. It was an average month.

Wills and the Texas Playboys evoked the image of the singing cowboy by dressing as cowboys, but whereas Gray's musicians had cowboy backgrounds, Wills's performers did not. Even in that, however, the Playboys were trend-setters. They affixed the cowboy image to western swing, and, inasmuch as their success encouraged a host of imitators, they rendered the clothing as acceptable as the music, even for people without appropriate antecedents. That the music had nothing whatsoever to do with cowboys is perhaps irrelevant. Postwar commercialism separated cowboy imagery in music from its historical roots anyway, and the Texas Playboys merely anticipated the process.

38

Others maintained the connection between cowboy clothes and cowboy music, however. The most famous of them all, surely, was Gene Autry, a Texan who grew up in Oklahoma and entered show business on the advice of Oklahoma's favorite son, Will Rogers.

It is a familiar story, and one that Autry has told many times: how he was working as a telegraph operator in the railroad station at Chelsea, Oklahoma; how he was strumming his guitar and singing, one summer night in 1927, when Will Rogers strolled in to send a wire; how Rogers listened to the song and then suggested that he go to New York and sing on the radio.

Autry did travel to New York, but he was not to sing on the radio. Instead, he received more advice: go home and get some experience. He made his debut on Tulsa's KVOO as "Oklahoma's Yodeling Cowboy" in 1928 with Jimmy Wilson's Catfish String Band (Wilson, incidentally, was one of the first performers to experiment with sound effects on radio). Autry traveled extensively throughout the state, singing at meetings, dances, and parties. In 1929 he returned to New York and made the first of many recordings, and in 1930 he began working for Chicago radio station WLS, in a job he held until 1934 when he moved to Hollywood to launch his movie career. He had ninety-three films to his credit when he retired from the screen in 1953.

Gene Autry sang in those films, and on "Gene Autry's Melody Ranch," his CBS network-radio program that began in 1940 and continued — with the same three-year pause for service in World War II that punctuated his movie career — until 1956. The television series he produced for CBS lasted from 1950 until 1956, and he sang there, too. Gene Autry made his last recordings in 1964, after nearly forty years of singing. He was by then a millionaire.

Jimmy Wakely, Johnny Bond, and Ray Whitley were singing cowboys whose careers intersected with Autry's. Wakely was born in Arkansas but grew up on a ranch in Oklahoma, where

Gene Autry

he learned to play the guitar. A talent-show appearance on Oklahoma City radio-station WKY marked the start of Wakely's career as a professional musician. In 1937 he formed the Wakely Trio, and the group secured a program on WKY. Gene Autry appeared as a guest on the show, liked what he heard, and signed the trio for his "Melody Ranch" program. That led eventually to Hollywood, but, while the trio backed Autry's singing on radio and on tours, it performed in only one Autry film, *Heart of the Rio Grande* (1942). Wakely, however, left the Autry camp and starred in two-dozen singing-cowboy epics of his own. He recorded throughout the 1940s, and in 1950 he made a series of hit records with Margaret Whiting, including "Let's Go to Church Next Sunday Morning." When author James Horwitz interviewed him in the mid-1970s, Wakely was living in North Hollywood, still encouraging people to go to church next Sunday morning, and making money as Gene Autry's partner in a mail-order record business.

Johnny Bond, born Cyrus Whitfield Bond in Enville, Oklahoma, in 1915, was a member of the Wakely Trio. He spent fourteen years as the comic relief on Autry's network radio show and performed in films and on television. As a boy growing up in Marietta, Oklahoma, Bond had ordered a ninety-eight-cent ukelele from a Montgomery Ward catalog, learned to play from instructions in an accompanying booklet, moved on to the guitar, and began performing on radio in Oklahoma City at the age of nineteen. His experience with Autry led to a recording contract with Columbia that produced such songs as "Oklahoma Waltz," "Cherokee Waltz," and "A Petal from a Faded Rose," and left him a long way from his ukelele days. In films Bond was somebody's sidekick—as opposed to the sort of hero portrayed by Autry or Wakely—and perhaps because of that, he received more exposure: he appeared in movies with Tex Ritter, Roy Rogers, and William Boyd, as well as with Autry.

Ray Whitley was a singing cowboy from Georgia whose principal claim to fame may be that he collaborated with Gene Autry on "I'm Back in the Saddle Again," still recognized as Autry's theme song. He built a reputation singing with his band at rodeos in New York and Boston and following the theater circuit in the northeast, in the figurative footsteps of Otto Gray. In the mid-1930s he began making Hollywood westerns, and in 1938 he received an invitation from Cousin Herald Goodman (formerly a member of the "Vagabonds," six years earlier the first group of professional musicians ever to appear on the Grand Ole Opry) to perform as a guest on Goodman's "Saddle Mountain Roundup" radio show on KVOO. Whitley was a guest who stayed, touring and performing with the Goodman cast from 1938 to 1940, with time off for rodeo appearances.

Whitley was a smash in Oklahoma—a real movie cowboy, live and in-person, and a singer to boot. This dual popularity had interesting repercussions. Everyone who went to the movies knew that cowboy heroes never married, but Whitley was not only married, he was a father as well. Ordinarily that might have presented no problems for the folks at KVOO, but wife Kay was part of Whitley's act. So, for two years in Tulsa, she was introduced to audiences as "Miss Kay Karson," or "Miss Kay Johnson," or just "Miss Kay." And she was supposed to be Whitley's *sister!*

On the road in Stillwater, Purcell, Pawhuska, Miami, Eufaula, and points between and beyond, the "Saddle Mountain Round-up" cast was billed as "The Southwest's Greatest Barn Dance Show," and adhered to a rigorous schedule. The performers did two radio programs a day during the week, one at the crack of dawn and another at noon, and then took off for a theater in some eastern-Oklahoma town. On Saturday nights the road show did hour-long remote broadcasts from wherever they happened to be.

Whitley left for California with his band—he would make a series of films with Tim Holt—aware of the growing popularity of western swing. He had, after all, two years to contemplate the success of Bob Wills. Whitley became an exponent of western swing, secured the services of fiddler and former Texas Playboy Jesse Ashlock, and toured the West Coast. As if he were not busy enough, Whitley also managed Jimmy Wakely's career for several months and appeared in some Wakely films. Even after television killed Hollywood's B-feature westerns in the 1950s, Whitley could still draw crowds who remembered him. He acted from time to time in television westerns, performed in Las Vegas nightclubs in the 1960s, and as recently as 1974—when he was seventy-three years old—appeared on the Grand Ole Opry.

The singing cowboy, in his various manifestations, was the central figure in rural white music in Oklahoma from the 1920s to the 1940s. But more than that, he was a principal exporter of southwestern popular culture to other parts of the country. He had a great deal to do also with shaping Oklahoma's image nationally, to which the existence of the National Cowboy Hall of Fame and Western Heritage Center in Oklahoma City and the pronouncements of the Oklahoma Tourism and Recreation Department attest. Oklahoma still harvests rewards from the efforts of its singing cowboys—and well it might, since Oklahoma's singing cowboys were the best in the business. A few have been forgotten, perhaps, but others are firmly entrenched in both the history of American music and in the popular imagination. Whatever they did for the reputation of the state, they did more for its people, developing, performing, and spreading the influence of a distinctive brand of music that, quite apart from its cultural significance, filled the air and made—in no small way—the hard years of the 1920s and 1930s easier to bear.

Sources

Brief biographies of most of the people mentioned here and in chapter 7 may be found in Irwin Stambler and Grelun Landon, *Encyclopedia of Folk, Country and Western Music* (New York: St. Martin's Press, 1969), and

Melvin Shestack, *The Country Music Encyclopedia* (New York: Thomas Y. Crowell Co., 1974). The relationships between singing cowboys and western swing are traced in Bill C. Malone, *Country Music, U.S.A.: A Fifty-Year History* (Austin: University of Texas Press, 1968), chap. 5, and Robert Shelton and Burt Goldblatt, *The Country Music Story: A Picture History of Country and Western Music* (Secaucus, N.J.: Castle Books, 1966), chap. 7. The Malone book is the best general introduction to the history of country music, and the Shelton-Goldblatt volume is considerably more than the title implies. Both discuss Otto Gray. See also William W. Savage, Jr., *The Cowboy Hero: His Image in American History and Culture* (Norman: University of Oklahoma Press, 1979), chap. 5.

In addition to the sources on Bob Wills cited in chapter 2, consult Charles R. Townsend's essay in Bill C. Malone and Judith McCulloh, eds., *Stars of Country Music: Uncle Dave Macon to Johnny Rodriguez* (Urbana: University of Illinois Press, 1975), pp. 157-78, and Bob Pinson, ed., "Bob Wills and His Texas Playboys on Radio, 1942," *The Journal of Country Music* 5, no. 4 (Winter 1974):134-93.

Gene Autry, *Back in the Saddle Again* (Garden City, N.Y.: Doubleday & Co., 1978), was ghostwritten by Mickey Herskowitz and is useful despite some internal contradictions. It should be supplemented by Douglas B. Green's essay on Autry in the Malone-McCulloh volume, pp. 142-56, which is based on information provided by Johnny Bond, Jimmy Wakely, and Ray Whitley, among others. James Horwitz, *They Went Thataway* (New York: E. P. Dutton & Co., 1976), contains material from interviews with Autry (pp. 172-87) and Jimmy Wakely (pp. 238-42), and the reader should not be put off by the fact that Horwitz misspells Wakely's name throughout. The principal source on Ray Whitley is Gerald F. Vaughn and Douglas B. Green, "A Singing Cowboy on the Road: A Look at the Performance Career of Ray Whitley," *The Journal of Country Music* 5, no. 1 (Spring 1974):3-16.

Relevant recordings include *Western Swing* (Old Timey 105), which contains several Bob Wills cuts from the period 1935-37, and *The Bob Wills Anthology* (Columbia PG 32416), a two-record set containing twenty-two Tulsa-era tunes. *Gene Autry's Country Music Hall of Fame Album* (Columbia CS 1035) features several singing-cowboy standards, together with "That Silver-haired Daddy of Mine," which Autry introduced over KVOO. *Gene Autry's Melody Ranch Radio Show* (Murray Hill 897296) is a four-record set of nine programs, including the first broadcast (which repeats the Will Rogers story), one show for each year from 1947 to 1953, and one 1956 program. Johnny Bond is featured on those sides and on *Best of Johnny Bond* (Harmony 7308). Representative are *Here's Jimmy Wakely* (Vocalion 73857) and *Singing Cowboy* (Shasta 522), a collection of standards from Wakely's radio broadcasts.

5. Wired for Sound:
Oklahoma and the Electric Guitar

THE guitar, an instrument of European origin, was effective only in solo performances or with small string ensembles, and, as the instrument grew in popularity in the seventeenth and eighteenth centuries, concert music written for it reflected that limitation. In the New World the guitar became important as a folk instrument, played to accompany singing, or for work in string bands. In brass-band or orchestral settings, the guitar was less useful because of its limited volume. The gut strings of the Old World gave way to the steel strings of the New World, but in either case the guitar produced notes of relatively brief duration and could not compete with the other instruments. Accordingly, early bands assigned the guitar a rhythm function, and guitarists played only in chords—for, striking the six strings at once with a plectrum, or pick, one might produce sufficient volume to be heard at least in the background. It was simply not loud enough to serve as a solo instrument.

People who played guitar and recognized its potential as a solo instrument also accepted the technological problem it posed. How might one amplify and sustain the guitar's notes and make it competitive, so to speak, with other musical instruments? Guitarists experimented with resonators, acoustical amplifiers that were merely elaborations on the principle of the megaphone, and with primitive electrical amplifiers manufactured from old telephone parts. One of the first of these experimenters was Eddie Durham, who played trombone and doubled on guitar for the Oklahoma City Blue Devils. Durham was probably the first jazz musician to play electric guitar, and most authorities agree that he has not received the credit he deserves as a pioneer developer of the instrument.

Eddie Durham was born in San Marcos, Texas, in 1906. As a teenager he found work in the Miller Brothers 101 Ranch Wild West show, headquartered near Ponca City. The show featured two bands, one the parade brass band that played for the audience attending the main exhibition, and a smaller band that played in a minstrel sideshow. The musicians were good, and they could read music better than Durham; but the young trombonist settled down to business and learned what he needed to know. He began to write arrangements (later in his career he would arrange for Basie and Glenn Miller) for the bandsmen, many of whom were looking for opportunities to hone their skills and to play something besides marches. On the road the 101 show generally closed at nine in the evening but stayed in town overnight before departing for the next stop on the tour. Some of the musicians decided they had time to organize dances during the layovers. The band leader asked them, "How can we have a dance when we ain't got no piano?" Durham wrote horn arrangements so the brass sounded pianolike. Saxophones were brought in from the minstrel show, and the dance band became a reality. The musicians would rent a hall, charge two bits for admission, and earn a couple of dollars apiece each night. And Eddie Durham had a chance to play jazz.

Durham left the 101 Ranch in 1926 and became an Okla-

Eddie Durham

homa City Blue Devil. The trombone was his bread and butter, and the guitar was his hobby. He experimented with the guitar as a Blue Devil and then with Bennie Moten; after Moten's death Durham found a job with Jimmie Lunceford's band and took up his duties in the brass section. His experiments fascinated Lunceford, who determined to use the guitar as a solo instrument. As Durham played, using a resonator, Lunceford would move a microphone close to the sound hole on the guitar to amplify the sustaining effect of the resonator. He was sufficiently impressed with the results to feature Durham as a soloist on a September, 1935, recording of "Hittin' the Bottle," perhaps the first record of an amplified guitar ever made in American jazz. Leonard Feather, the jazz authority, claims that it was perhaps the first recording of any kind to feature an amplified guitar, but, as we shall see, that was not the case.

The Durham-Lunceford technology, crude though it was, took the guitar from the rhythm section of jazz bands and made it available to musicians in a dynamic and exciting form, suitable for solo work. The performer who, more than any other, would demonstrate the efficacy of the new instrument and its promise for the future of American jazz was a young man from Oklahoma City named Charles Christian.

Born in Bonham, Texas, in 1916, Charlie Christian grew up in Oklahoma City and learned to play the guitar from his father, a blind street singer. Christian, his father, and his brothers augmented the family income by wandering through middle-class white neighborhoods playing selections upon request from a widely varied musical repertoire. Christian's brother Edward studied music—as Jimmy Rushing had—at Douglass High School, played in the band, performed in school productions of light opera, and eventually formed his own group, occasionally sitting in (he played piano and bass) with Oran Page and some of the other Blue Devils. Charles, meanwhile, fash-

48

ioned guitarlike instruments from cigar boxes in his manual arts classes at Douglass—when he consented to attend school at all—and he and brother Clarence often impressed classmates with their facile playing on the handmade instruments. The frequently truant Christian would appear in the school yard, begin to perform, and draw a large crowd. The principal's intervention was necessary to prompt the students to return to class.

Eddie Christian's group, of which Charlie was a member, played weekends at local barbecues, setting up a bandstand and sending Melvin Moore, the vocalist, into the crowd to collect donations. The five musicians would make perhaps seventeen dollars a night. "Then," recalled Moore, "Charlie got so it was a case of three-for-me-and-one-for-you, and everybody got mad." The group dissolved for a while, but Charlie Christian performed with other bands around Oklahoma City. By 1934 he was playing bass with Alphonso Trent's sextet; later, he performed on guitar with the Jeter-Pillars Orchestra in Saint Louis. Back in Oklahoma City in 1937, Christian was going nowhere fast. That was when Eddie Durham came to town.

Durham was there with Basie, whose band he had joined a few months earlier. He had by then acquired an electric guitar—a small company made it for him, since electric guitars were not in large-scale production at that time and were not available to the general public—and he was learning to cope with the difficulties it presented to the traveling musician. The instrument required alternating current in a period when direct current was what most wall sockets produced. And proprietors of dance halls were skeptical of the thing, fearing it would short-circuit their lights. It was new enough to be strange, and some people wondered why anyone would want to play it. Because it was wired, perhaps spectators feared for the life of the performer.

Charlie Christian was playing a decrepit guitar of ancient vintage when Durham met him. He had never seen an electric guitar before, or so Durham guessed. Durham showed him some playing techniques and later remarked that he had never met anyone who learned as rapidly as Christian did. In 1938, when electric guitars began to appear on the market, Christian bought one and joined Trent's band again.

Durham taught Christian, and so did Jim Daddy Walker, a Kansas City guitarist who performed with Jap Allen's band, a group once based in Tulsa and often seen in Oklahoma. Two years Christian's senior, Walker strongly influenced the young guitarist's development. Except for that influence, history might well have forgotten the older man. Jim Daddy Walker died in Kansas City in 1949 at the age of thirty-five. That was a little more than seven years after his star pupil died in New York City at the age of twenty-six.

According to Ralph Ellison, Charlie Christian died of tuberculosis contracted in the wooden Oklahoma City slum tenement where he grew up. That is an oversimplification. John Hammond has noted that Christian was making good progress in his fight against the disease in Staten Island's Seaview Hospital in mid-February, 1942, when another musician smuggled the guitarist a quantity of marijuana and some female companionship. Thereafter, Christian's condition worsened, and he died on March 2. What is not in question is that when he died, he was an internationally prominent musician and perhaps (if one wishes to argue about Belgian guitarist Django Reinhardt) the foremost jazz guitarist. That fame had come to him in three short years.

John Hammond, jazz critic and in the late 1930s a columnist for *Down Beat* magazine, discovered Charlie Christian with Trent's band—just as he had discovered so many others in places where few remembered to look—and recommended him to Benny Goodman. Goodman had broken the color line in 1935 and was one of the few white jazzmen to hire black musicians and thus to appear in public with an integrated band. Christian joined Goodman in September, 1939, two years after having seen his first electric guitar.

Charlie Christian

Performing with the Goodman Sextet and occasionally with the full Goodman orchestra, Charlie Christian introduced jazz audiences to single-string solos on the amplified guitar. In after-hours sessions at Minton's Playhouse on 118th Street in Harlem, where Dizzy Gillespie, Thelonious Monk, and Charlie Parker jammed with old Blue Devils like Basie, Lester Young, and Ben Webster and built modern American jazz, the Christian kid from Oklahoma, almost scat-singing to accompany the cascade of notes from his instrument ("be-bop, be-bop, be-bop"), gave a name to the new music of the 1940s. And too soon he died. Critics said, and say yet, that the Christian kid from Oklahoma was the best there ever was.

Charlie Christian, despite his brief career and the relatively few recordings he made, exerted a profound influence on guitarists who arrived later on the jazz scene. Billy Bauer, Al Hendrickson, Charlie Byrd, Tiger Haynes, Sal Salvador, Willie Harris, Tal Farlow, Tiny Grimes, Jimmy Raney, Mary Osborne, Joseph Barry Galbraith, and Kenny Burrell, for all their musical diversity and their differing regional origins, could cite Charlie Christian as a force in their musical lives. But perhaps the name most closely linked with Christian's is that of another Oklahoman, Barney Kessel, who is frequently mentioned as the principal exponent of Christian's musical style. Again, that is an over-simplification.

Barney Kessel was born in Muskogee in 1923. He taught himself to play the guitar, and at the age of thirteen he was performing with local musicians. There were several bands in town in 1936, staffed by professional musicians who had retired from life on the road and for whom performing had become a weekend pastime. There were white groups, led by Frater Greer and Jo Harris and Don Farthing; there were black groups, led by John Maddox and Ellis Ezell. Most of the time, young Kessel played with Ezell's band and was its only white performer. The white groups played stock arrangements, and that did not appeal to Kessel. Blacks, he said, played more interesting music, music possessed of a richness in melody, rhythm, and harmony. If this opinion was early evidence of independent thinking, it would be characteristic of a good many of Kessel's subsequent career decisions.

Barney Kessel left Muskogee in the early summer of 1942, and things began to happen for him. He joined the orchestra that drummer Ben Pollack had organized in 1941 to back Chico Marx's visually remarkable piano stylings. In 1944 he worked on the soundtrack for (and appeared briefly in) a motion picture entitled *Jammin' the Blues*. Beginning in 1945 he performed with Charlie Barnet's orchestra, Hal McIntyre's dance band, and Artie Shaw's orchestra. In 1947 he was one of Lionel Hampton's "All-Stars" for a Gene Norman "Just Jazz" concert in Pasadena.

Leonard Feather interviewed Kessel early in his career and asked about the musicians whose work had influenced the guitarist. Kessel mentioned Charlie Christian. He also mentioned Louis Armstrong, Lester Young, Roy Eldridge, Nat ("King") Cole, Claude Debussy, and Maurice Ravel. Perhaps Feather thought the list incongruous. Perhaps the idea of an Oklahoma connection seemed too good to ignore. Whatever the case, Feather omitted the two trumpet players, the saxophonist, the pianist, and the French composers and wrote of Kessel as the heir apparent to Charlie Christian. Never mind that the first recording young Barney Kessel ever saved his money to buy was the work of the Budapest String Quartet: Kessel was Christian's leading disciple.

When he was sixteen years old, Kessel spent three days playing guitar in Oklahoma City with Charlie Christian. It was a valuable experience. Kessel learned that Christian could not read music, could not finger the guitar correctly, and seldom spoke except in grunts. Christian was kind and helpful and encouraging. And Kessel learned that to grow musically you have to be yourself. He had, to the age of sixteen, been copying

Charlie Christian, and during those three days in Oklahoma City he found that all he could play was the music he had heard Christian play. He learned that one may only use the work of others as a point of departure, and it was a lesson he never forgot.

Kessel worked in radio and as a studio musician, and in the early 1950s he toured overseas with the Oscar Peterson Trio. In 1954 he began a prolonged stint as a studio musician and free-lancer in films, on television, and for recording sessions. Variously, he served as music director for the early Bob Crosby television programs, "artists and repertoire" man for Verve records, and as one of the jazzmen on John Cassavetes's *Johnny Staccato* television series. His recordings with Ben Webster, Lionel Hampton, Oscar Peterson, Julie London, Roy Eldridge, Billy Holiday, Woody Herman, Red Norvo, and many others kept him ranked at the top (or near it) in national and international jazz polls in the 1950s and 1960s. By the mid-1960s, in addition to his studio work, he was writing about the guitar and making plans to produce his own records. He risked outraging jazz critics and other purists by playing television commercials and as an instrumentalist on a number of rock-and-roll records.

Kessel recorded soundtracks for four Elvis Presley films, including *Blue Hawaii* (1961) and *Fun in Acapulco* (1963). He was an instrumentalist on the Righteous Brothers' hit of 1965 "You've Lost that Lovin' Feelin'," and on the Beach Boys' "Good Vibrations" (1966). He recorded with soul artists Joe Tex and Ike and Tina Turner. In the late 1960s he made seventy-one five-minute devotional television programs with Mahalia Jackson and played on her recordings for Columbia. It was all in a decade's work. Kessel's versatility and flexibility has allowed him to record with Judy Garland, Barbara Streisand, and Tex Ritter; Marlene Dietrich and Gene Autry; Stan Kenton and Lawrence Welk; and Dinah Shore and Dinah Washington.

Barney Kessel

Variety, to Kessel, meant personal growth. But all the while, he expressed a desire to leave the rat race, to travel more, and to return to the jazz scene. By 1970 he was practically unknown to younger jazz audiences and almost absent from record catalogs. He was tired of studio work, and he was not recording his own music because of the limitations of record companies: large companies could pay artists, but they imposed restrictions on them; small companies that allowed artistic freedom had inadequate distribution and did not make money. So Kessel began working club dates and performing in Europe. He began thinking of his music as improvisation rather than jazz.

On any list of significant contributors to the development of American jazz, the names of Charlie Christian and Barney Kessel will appear. Together they form a strong entry from Oklahoma and extend the state's reputation as a matrix for jazz music. The early careers of both men illustrate the dynamism of Oklahoma's cultural environment in the 1920s and 1930s. Coming from different backgrounds and different traditions, they nevertheless had their music in common. They could point to similar influences—both admired, for example, the music of Lester Young—and in a real sense they had similar cultural roots.

Coming from yet another tradition was Bob Dunn, whose contributions to the development of the amplified guitar surpassed even those of Eddie Durham. But to understand what Dunn accomplished, one must consider briefly a bit of the musical history of Hawaii.

Hawaiians acquired the guitar originally from European sailors, but instead of plucking or strumming the instrument in the traditional European manner, Hawaiians placed it flat in the lap and fretted it, not with the fingers but with a smooth, hard "slide" made of bone and later of metal. In rural America both black and white musicians played in a similar style, slack-tuning the guitar to an open chord and using the necks of glass bottles or perhaps pocketknife blades for slides. But it was not a style that attracted much attention until World War I, when Hawaiian musicians touring the United States popularized it.

Bob Dunn had grown up listening to his father's fiddle music in the family's home near Braggs, a few miles southeast of Muskogee. He heard a group of touring Hawaiians perform in Kusa, near Henryetta, in 1917. Fascinated by the Hawaiian guitar, Dunn took the trouble to acquire one, studied the instrument by correspondence (with a bona fide Hawaiian musician named Walter Kolomoku), and subsequently joined the Panhandle Cowboys and Indians, an Oklahoma band with which he performed from 1927 to 1934. These were years when the national flirtation with the Hawaiian instrument took on the proportions of an affair, nowhere more noticeable than in country music. A California company began manufacturing the Dobro guitar in 1925 to capitalize on the popularity of the Hawaiian style. It was an acoustical instrument, of course, and for band work it faced the same limitations of any unamplified guitar.

Late in 1934, Bob Dunn left the Panhandle Cowboys and Indians for a job with Milton Brown and His Musical Brownies, a popular string band featured on KTAT radio, in Fort Worth. Brown's band, formed in 1932, played white jazz—western-swinger Brown was, like Bob Wills, an alumnus of the Light Crust Doughboys, the prototype of southwestern dance bands—and that suited Bob Dunn. During the next few months, the newest Musical Brownie set about modernizing the Hawaiian guitar and making it a jazz instrument. He bought a standard flattop guitar, raised and magnetized the strings, attached an electrical pickup, and plugged the whole thing into an amplifier (amplifiers were commercially available by 1934). Dunn played the instrument flat, in the Hawaiian style. He used it for a Chicago recording session with Milton Brown in January,

1935. That was eight months before Eddie Durham made his historic recording with the Jimmie Lunceford band.

The chronology of all this is interesting. Jazz is usually thought to be an older idiom than commercial country music—those turn-of-the-century New Orleans antecedents are probably responsible for that—yet Dunn's work preceded Durham's. But in the 1930s, what distinctions could be made between jazz and commercial country music? Barney Kessel believed that jazz had a sophistication lacking in western swing and that white bandleaders frustrated their musicians by making them play dance music. Bob Wills, according to Kessel, insisted on playing music beneath the level of his jazz-oriented instrumentalists. Perhaps so, but the data still indicate that the biggest hit Milton Brown and His Musical Brownies ever had was "St. Louis Blues," and information like that tends to blur distinctions. In any case, the discussion may be less important than that there were many Oklahomans, or persons with strong Oklahoma connections, involved in changing both the substance and the sound of American music. A couple of them may even have invented the electric guitar.

Sources

Eddie Durham's recollections of the early history of the amplified guitar and his meeting with Charlie Christian are found in Leonard Feather, *The Book of Jazz: From Then Till Now,* rev. ed. (New York: Dell Publishing Co., 1976), chap. 12. Ralph Ellison, *Shadow and Act,* pp. 233-40, discusses Christian's beginnings in Oklahoma City. Melvin Moore's recollections are contained in Dance, *The World of Count Basie,* pp. 341-43. Barney Kessel spoke with me on October 13, 1980. See also Bill Lee, "Barney Kessel," in *The Guitar Player Book* (New York: Grove Press, 1978), pp. 117-20. Bob Dunn's contributions to guitar amplification are discussed in Bill C. Malone, *Country Music, U.S.A.,* chap. 5.

Some Durham guitar solos may be heard on Jimmie Lunceford, *Harlem Shout* (MCA-1305), which also contains a few Durham arrangements. The best collection of Christian's recordings is *Solo Flight: The Genius of Charlie Christian* (Columbia CG 30779). Kessel is where you find him, and he is likely to be found on any number of jazz recordings. Portions of the "Just Jazz" Concert of 1947 are featured on Lionel Hampton, *The "Original" Star Dust* (MCA-198), which is a good example of early Kessel. His work with Oscar Peterson may be sampled on two sides of Roy Eldridge, *Dale's Wail* (Verve VE-2-2531). *The Barney Kessel Quartet: Workin' Out!* (Contemporary S 7585) dates from the early 1960s and is the first recording by Kessel as the leader of his own group. Of his work in the mid-1970s, *Barney Plays Kessel* (Concord CJ9), for which he composed all the music, is representative. A superb recent Kessel recording is *Jellybeans* (Concord CJ-164). Dunn's solos are featured on Milton Brown and His Musical Brownies, *Taking Off* (String STR 804). Of interest also is *Devil with the Devil* (Rambler 102), which features several 1930s western swing groups, including Brown (with Dunn), the Light Crust Dough-boys, and Jimmie Revard and His Oklahoma Playboys, a band based in San Antonio. *Fifty Years of Jazz Guitar* (Columbia CG 33566) contains an example from 1929 of Hawaiian guitar played by Hawaiians, songs by Durham and Christian, and the Bob Wills version of "White Heat," featuring Wills's steel guitarist, Leon McAuliff. Time-Life Records' *The Guitarists* (STL-J12), in the *Giants of Jazz* series discussed in the sources for chapter 8, contains much Christian and Durham material and includes biographical notes that correct much of what was known about Christian's life. *John Hammond on Record: An Autobiography* discusses Christian in chapters 24 and 25.

6. Woody and the World

H E has been likened to Walt Whitman. He has been called America's Robert Burns. John Greenway said he was "the greatest figure in American folksong," and Louis Adamic labeled his compositions "the living folk songs of America." To Pete Seeger he was a national folk poet, and to Studs Terkel he was the "champion of all American ballad writers." A secretary of the interior said Americans were fortunate to have his music. Will Geer said one of his songs should become the national anthem.

Oklahoma history books have said nothing about him at all. Perhaps he knew that would happen when he sang, "I Ain't Got No Home in This World Anymore."

Woodrow Wilson Guthrie was born in Okemah, Oklahoma, on July 14, 1912, and grew up hearing music. His mother sang the ballads she had learned from her British parents and taught them to her children. His father, a Texan, knew the guitar and banjo and had performed with cowboy bands before giving up music for family and a career in real estate. Guthrie heard these songs and more besides. There was black music and Indian music, there were spirituals and coal miners' songs, and there were all the tunes from all the places people had left to move to the oil boomtown of Okemah. Young Guthrie sold newspapers on the street, earning pennies from passers-by for dancing jigs and singing songs—some old, some new—that he had learned in the boisterous community: "Dream of the Miner's Child," "Soldier's Sweetheart," "Barbara Allen," "Drunkard's Dream," songs about the Titanic, songs about the Hindenburg.

Great personal tragedy marked Guthrie's childhood. A sister burned to death, his mother was committed to the state hospital in Norman, and his father was critically injured in another fire. The Guthrie children were separated and sent to live in foster homes. By the time he was seventeen, Woody was ready for other things—a foster mother had set him to the task of supervising the activities of her pet hen—and he left Okemah to become that for which there are many euphemisms: a hobo.

Guthrie traveled first to Texas, where he sang, danced, played his harmonica, and increased his repertoire by listening to the music of those he met. He and a fiddle-playing uncle performed at parties, dances, rodeos, carnivals, and an occasional banquet, and Guthrie met and married the first of his three wives. He then moved to California and performed with his cousin, Jack Guthrie, a cowboy singer remembered for recording Woody's "Oklahoma Hills." He also sang on Los Angeles radio-station KFVD with a female partner named Lefty Lou Crissman, and the duo received twenty-thousand pieces of fan mail during the two years that "Woody and Lefty Lou" were on the air. Beginning in the late 1930s, and until he joined the Merchant Marine in 1943, Guthrie divided his time between California and New York, with intermediate stops in Oklahoma to visit family and friends.

Folksinger Pete Seeger met Guthrie in New York in 1939 at a benefit performance for migrant workers, whose plight John Steinbeck had recently publicized in *The Grapes of Wrath*. He

61

was, Seeger recalled years later, a small man in cowboy clothes, and he needed a shave. By his own admission, Seeger was an eastern snob who thought that nothing worthwhile existed west of the Hudson River. Guthrie encouraged him to see the country, taught him to hitchhike and hobo, and helped him learn to talk to what Seeger called "ordinary" people. It was an education.

Shortly before World War II, Guthrie, Seeger, Lee Hays, and Millard Lampell formed the Almanac Singers, a group in many ways the prototype of the folk-music aggregations that would become popular (and fashionable) after the war. Occasionally, Burl Ives joined the group for concerts in New York, and on tours such musicians as Josh White and Cisco Houston performed with them. The Almanac Singers had a fluctuating membership. Sometimes only Guthrie and Seeger were members, and at other times there were more. The group's collective interests seemed to reside with the problems of workers, and to that end they sang a good many pro-labor-union songs, intermixed with traditional material. They also sang antiwar songs.

Before the late 1930s, Woody Guthrie could be conveniently dismissed by any who disliked his music as just another hillbilly singer, a migrating Okie with a coarse voice and an almost primitive guitar style. But New York brought new status. To audiences he was not a hillbilly singer—they would not patronize concerts by hillbilly musicians—but a folksinger, something altogether different and something acceptable. By eastern definitions Woody Guthrie had the necessary credentials.

If Guthrie's life made him an "original" in the eyes of his eastern fans, so did his behavior. Pete Seeger remembered him as being honest to the point of rudeness. Guthrie made no apologies for himself, his appearance, or his demeanor, and Seeger compared him to Popeye: he was what he was, and that is all he was. He drank and swore, traveled when he pleased, and stayed where he pleased. Seeger did not mention it, but others remember Guthrie as quite the womanizer. He forgot to pay his bills, ruined hosts' sheets by sleeping with his boots on, and generally made life difficult for his family and his friends. Patrons of the arts, if they do not admire that sort of thing, at least accept it as an example of the eccentricity of genius. And Guthrie was undeniably a genius.

After his stint in the Merchant Marine, Woody Guthrie returned to New York to continue his concerts and to begin recording for Moses Asch, the founder of Folkways Records. In the early 1950s he was hospitalized, suffering from Huntington's chorea, a progressive nervous disorder that is hereditary. It was probably the same disease that afflicted his mother. Guthrie's own deterioration was slow. The disease took fifteen years to break the hardy constitution fashioned by riding in boxcars, sleeping under bridges and in migrant camps, and moving among the American people. But it was inexorable. Woodrow Wilson Guthrie died in a New Jersey hospital on October 4, 1967, at the age of fifty-five.

Between 1935 and 1950, when most of his songs were written, Guthrie spoke out against any number of perceived evils; that is, anything standing between a man and his family finding what they needed to get through the day: a place to live, food to eat, clothes to wear, and work to earn the money to pay for it all. He was a country boy (though often come to town) without rural or even regional prejudices, and people in trouble were all the same to him. Whether they hailed from a city or from a farm was irrelevant. People in trouble were generally victims of some corporate or bureaucratic injustice and thus could not share in the benefits of technology and industrialization. Or so thought Woody Guthrie. A small sign, affixed to his Gibson guitar just above the fret board near the sound hole, where all could read it while he played, neatly summarized his philosophy. It said, "This Machine Kills Fascists."

Laying about in all directions at perceived evils and broadly defining fascism to include corporate activity will give one's protests on behalf of the common folk a political character, and Woody Guthrie's work certainly had that, though not by his design. He had traveled extensively, had associated with all sorts of people, had listened to their problems and observed their lives, and had absorbed firsthand the chaotic images of the Dust Bowl and the misery of the Depression. He was not content merely to observe the privations and hardships of that era and describe them in his songs. Rather, he sought to respond, to try to make things better somehow. Guthrie did what he did best. He publicized problems in the hope that persons with resources greater than his own would also respond. It was inevitable that he would offend someone. The villains in some of Guthrie's pieces called him a Communist. Some, especially in Oklahoma, still call him one, and the label apparently has been sufficient to expel him from the histories of his native state. It has been said before, but it bears repeating because so few seem to listen: there is not one shred of evidence that Woody Guthrie was a Communist, or that he even cared in any significant way about organized political groups of any variety.

Woody Guthrie was a publicist, and as such he took advantage of any forum offered him. So he sang for Communists. So he wrote occasionally for *The Daily Worker*—or *The Sabbath Employee,* as he preferred to call it. And he scribbled in notebooks and on the backs of old envelopes—song lyrics, poems, random thoughts. He wrote letters to people. He drew cartoons with captions like "He Who Don't Register [to vote] Is Lost" and "Trouble Ain't Worth Nothing So I Won't Charge Nothing to Fix It." He sang for labor unions, tenant-farmer unions, college students, sailors, migrants, socialites, and anybody else who wanted music. He wrote more than a thousand songs because he had things to say and because others who had things to say hired him to do it for them. Thus, he praised rural electrification for the federal government and mourned Sacco and Vanzetti for Moses Asch. He never made much money at any of those things, but he was never without an idea or an audience.

Regardless of why they were written, Guthrie's songs are valuable as social history. His "Dust Bowl Ballads" are splendid descriptions of dust storms and people's reactions to them, the hardships faced by emigrants, the difficulties of travel, and the widespread optimism about the promise of California. Guthrie's songs from this period also reveal much about the attitudes of the economically distressed and Guthrie's own awareness of their needs. He injected wit, just as Will Rogers did in responses to the Depression, but Guthrie's humor carried sharper barbs. In his song "The Jolly Banker," for example, Guthrie observed that managers of fiscal institutions would, in response to the plight of borrowers brought on by hard times, "come down and help you, . . . rape you, . . . scalp you, singing, 'I'm a jolly banker, jolly banker am I.'" That was a fact of life to people Guthrie had known, and experience taught them to expect nothing else.

Several of Guthrie's songs were written specifically for the suffering population, and they indicate that Woody Guthrie did exactly what every bard and minstrel has done since the beginning of human history to inspire listeners who await better days. That is, he invented heroes.

Woody Guthrie's heroes were outlaws, people who fought the system and sometimes lost, but who always (at least in the songs) served as good examples of kindness, generosity, and, above all, humanity. They were Robin Hood types, identified the world over by historian Eric Hobsbawm as social bandits. As champions of impoverished rural populations, they robbed from the rich and gave to the poor. Regardless of whether or not they actually existed, the hint of their presence and the suggestion of their deeds offered hope to the disinherited. Guthrie took Steinbeck's Tom Joad and sang of him as a rural outlaw, a disciple of Preacher Casey (who believed that everybody was "just one big soul"), and a fighter for the rights of starving children.

He did much the same thing with Charles Arthur Floyd, by any measure of history a murderer, bank robber, and devotee of the low life. But who could be inspired by a song containing that sort of information? Instead, Guthrie's Pretty Boy Floyd robbed bankers who oppressed farmers, paid off mortgages on the homes of needy folk, left food baskets for families on relief, and paid for meals eaten in farmhouse kitchens by leaving thousand-dollar bills under napkins. Unlike bankers, Guthrie suggested, outlaws would never force families from their homes. Jesus Christ was another Guthrie outlaw, a working man who encouraged those with money to give generously to those who had none. He was a popular rural leader whose crucifixion was engineered by landlords, police, soldiers, and bankers—precisely the types who made life tough for Guthrie's listeners.

The outlaw construct was fantastic, of course, but that was a time of fantasy. The evident impotence of government and business to relieve economic distress accounted for the appearance of Tarzan and Superman in the comics (formerly, they were the funnies, but few things seemed funny in the 1930s), the popularity of *Gold Diggers of 1933* in movie theaters, and the origins of Buck Rogers and Captain Midnight on radio—all cultural responses to make things more bearable. In its own way, the image of the rural outlaw offered at least as many possibilities for psychological escapism as any afforded by spacemen or lords of the jungle.

The utility of Guthrie's music endured beyond the Depression. The songs have been described as timeless, and perhaps they are. But even if they are not—which would mean that the public would forget them—they will exist to be consulted for their view of a historical period, its people, places, and philosophies, and for their significance as sources of regional culture.

Woody Guthrie was a mediocre musician—he preferred, in the best folk tradition, to borrow tunes rather than compose them—but as a lyricist he was second to none. There is power in his words to evoke images and emotions, and "This Land Is Your Land," "Pastures of Plenty," and many other songs are evidence of it. His songs lack the complication of abstraction, and they require no special skills or preparation to perform. They were written to be sung, and sung they have been—by nearly everyone at some time or another. Guthrie's songs speak volumes about the relationship between genius and simplicity.

Woody Guthrie influenced American popular music in many ways. He was a guiding spirit behind the folk music revival of the 1950s, and his example fueled the topical balladry of the 1960s, from which popular music has not yet fully recovered. His music, no less than his personal history, inspired a new generation of songwriters that included Peter LaFarge, Bob Dylan, and Tom Paxton—people Pete Seeger preferred to call "Woody's Children."

Tom Paxton grew up in Bristow and studied drama at the University of Oklahoma. He was graduated in 1959 at the age of twenty-two, entered the army for six months, and returned to civilian life with a desire to become a singer and composer. In the early 1960s he was perhaps the most prolific songwriter of the new folk generation, numbering among his compositions "What Did You Learn in School?" and "The Willing Conscript" and "Ramblin' Boy." Paxton wrote protest songs, antiwar ditties that were more wry than angry but that nevertheless struck directly at hypocrisy Paxton observed at the core of hallowed

67

Woody Guthrie

American institutions.[1] "What Did You Learn in School?" considers public education as indoctrination, for example, and summarizes a child's daily lessons: the government is never wrong, capital punishment prevents crime, politicians are always fine men, and war has much to commend it. His songs were published in such magazines as *Broadside* (the brainchild of another Oklahoma singer and songwriter, Sis Cunningham, who had performed in the state in the 1930s with the Red Dust Players and worked with the Southern Tenant Farmers Union as an organizer) and *Sing Out!*, where they appeared with pro-civil-rights songs by Ernie Marrs, also from Bristow. Indeed, there were so many Oklahoma heirs to Woody Guthrie's ballad legacy that Gordon Friesen once wondered in *Sing Out!* whether or not there was a secret ingredient in the soil of eastern Oklahoma.

Tom Paxton returned to Oklahoma for the First Annual Woody Guthrie Folk Festival on July 22, 1979. He sang a clever but chilling song about the nuclear accident at Three Mile Island. In the wake of the furor over the death of Karen Silkwood, that might have been an unpopular thing to do in some quarters of Oklahoma, but it was appropriate to the occasion. "Woody, above all, gave us courage," Paxton had said in 1963. "He taught us that we can't run fast enough or far enough to stay out of trouble if we are going to be honest in our writing. Woody taught us that there comes a time when we've got to stand up and say 'Whoa!, we've run far enough.'" It was, in any case, the last Annual Woody Guthrie Folk Festival.

In time, the textbooks may be rewritten. In time, the chapters on Oklahoma culture may acknowledge America's Robert Burns.

---

[1] He also wrote love songs. His composition, "The Last Thing on My Mind," was a standard of the mid-1960s and was recorded by a number of pop artists.

Sources

The standard biography is Joe Klein, *Woody Guthrie: A Life* (New York: Alfred A. Knopf, 1980), which is also a superb book about Oklahoma and America. Guthrie's autobiography, *Bound for Glory* (New York: E. P. Dutton & Co., 1943), may be supplemented by a long piece entitled "My Life" in Moses Asch, ed., *American Folksong: Woody Guthrie,* new ed. (New York: Oak Publications, 1961), a book containing the texts of twenty-eight of Guthrie's songs. Woody Guthrie, *Born to Win,* ed. Robert Shelton (New York: Collier Books, 1967), is a collection of poetry, prose, letters, and artwork valuable for its insights into Guthrie's personality. Pete Seeger, "Woody Guthrie—Some Reminiscences," *Sing Out!,* July 1964, pp. 25-29, is an honest statement, but Studs Terkel "His Land Is Our Land," *American Way,* October 1976, pp. 8-12, is fawning. Essential to an understanding of Guthrie's childhood is Harry Menig, "Woody Guthrie: The Oklahoma Years, 1912-1929," *Chronicles of Oklahoma* 53 (Summer 1975):239-65. William W. Savage, Jr., "Rural Images, Rural Values and American Culture: A Comment," in Green, ed., *Rural Oklahoma,* pp. 113-27, discusses Guthrie's work, and especially his outlaw ballads, in the context of rural imagery, and Bob Gregory, "Was This Land Your Land, Woody?" *Oklahoma Monthly,* February 1977, pp. 37-44, describes attitudes about Guthrie in his hometown. A thoughtful assessment is John Greenway, "Woody Guthrie: The Man, the Land, the Understanding," in David A. DeTurk and A. Poulin, Jr., *The American Folk Scene: Dimensions of the Folksong Revival* (New York: Dell Publishing Co., 1967), pp. 184-202. Guthrie's musical "children" are the subjects of Gordon Friesen, "Something New Has Been Added," *Sing Out!,* October-November 1963, pp. 12-23, which is also the source of the Paxton quotation.

The one indispensable album is *Woody Guthrie: Library of Congress Recordings* (Elektra EKL-271/272), a three-disc set containing interviews recorded by folklorist Alan Lomax in March, 1940. Guthrie alternately reminisces and performs twenty-eight songs and instrumentals, including traditional materials and such Guthrie compositions as "Jolly Banker," "They Laid Jesus Christ in His Grave," and "Los Angeles New Year's Flood." Guthrie's topical songs may be heard on *Dust Bowl Ballads* (RCA LPV-502) and *This Land Is Your Land* (Folkways FTS 31001). His repertoire of traditional music is suggested by *Cowboy Songs* (Stinson SLP 32), recorded with Cisco Houston, and *Poor Boy* (Folkways 31010), with Houston and Sonny Terry.

Pete Seeger Sings Little Boxes & Other Broadsides (Verve/Folkways FV 9020) contains songs written by Tom Paxton and Ernie Marrs. Paxton's *Ain't That News* (Elektra 7-277) features some 1960s antiwar material, and *How Come the Sun* (Reprise RS 6443) suggested that he had mellowed in the early 1970s. But *Heroes* (Vanguard VSD-79411) and *New Songs from the Briarpatch* (Vanguard VSD-79395) revealed that the fires still burned. *The Paxton Report* (Mountain Railroad MR 52796) contains jabs at everything from the Chrysler Corporation loan to Henry Kissinger to wife-beating. Sis Cunningham's work, including her classic "How Can You Keep on Movin'," may be sampled on *Sundown* (Folkways FH 5319), which adds another perspective to the social history of Oklahoma in the 1930s.

See the sources on Bob Dylan listed for chapter 2. Dylan's musical tribute to Guthrie is "Song to Woody" on *Bob Dylan* (Columbia 8579). Of interest also is Willis Alan Ramsey's "Boy from Oklahoma" on *Willis Alan Ramsey* (Shelter SRL 52013).

7. Country Ladies and Gentlemen

COUNTRY-AND-WESTERN music has been an important part of Oklahoma's popular culture for more than half a century because it is a musical genre appealing to rural white audiences, and Oklahoma has been historically a predominantly white and largely rural state. Country-and-western music is a commercialized form of rural white folk music, which, as we have seen, grew from the British ballad tradition and moved to Oklahoma as a reflection of the cultural influences of the upper South. We have also noted a part of its development from the cowboy string bands of people like Otto Gray to the western-swing groups of Bob Wills and others.

During the decades 1910-19 and 1930-39, Oklahoma produced large numbers of country-and-western musicians—numbers out of all proportion to the state's relatively small population. Music researchers Richard A. Peterson and Russell Davis, Jr., have suggested that the musicians born in the first decade were generally those who achieved their fame playing western swing, while musicians born during the 1930s generally were taken as children to other parts of the country by parents seeking to escape the Dust Bowl or to find work in defense plants. Only Arkansas and Louisiana (combined by Peterson and Davis for statistical analysis) and Texas produced a comparable number of musicians in the Southwest, but those states had a population base larger than Oklahoma's.

The numbers alone might be expected to confirm the importance of the music to Oklahoma's cultural environment, but Peterson and Davis suggested only a part of the story. They considered emigration in the 1930s, for example, but not immigration: Nearly every Oklahoma-born musician who left the state was replaced by another one who arrived from somewhere else. This shuffling about (immigrants usually came from no great distance) in most cases merely underscored the cultural continuity of the region. Elton Britt, for example, though born in Arkansas in 1917, grew up in northeastern Oklahoma and absorbed its musical traditions at dances, parties, and family sings, developing a style and repertoire that impressed talent scouts and led to a contract with Los Angeles radio-station KMPC in 1932 and one with RCA Victor in 1937. In twenty-two years with RCA, Britt disseminated those rural Oklahoma traditions through 56 albums and 672 single releases.

Nor does a statistical profile explain the extension of a regional culture into other parts of the country. The westward migration of thousands of Oklahomans during the 1930s resulted in the appearance of enclaves of Oklahoma culture all along the way. The area around Bakersfield, California, was home to many who fled hard times in Oklahoma, drawn west, as Woody Guthrie said, by the imagery of Jimmie Rodgers's song, "California Blues"—fair weather, water like cherry wine, and so forth. Two Oklahomans who reached Bakersfield were Jim and Flossie Haggard, who left Checotah for the west in 1935 in a nine-year-old Chevrolet, but only after the barn had burned and drought had killed their crops. Their son, Merle, was born in Bakersfield in 1937.

The Haggard family lived in a converted boxcar. They may not have had much, but they had music. Father and grandfather were eastern Oklahoma fiddlers, although his wife's devotion to the Church of Christ had led Jim Haggard to give up performing in roadhouses and honky-tonks. Merle began playing guitar at the age of eleven. Each Saturday night he listened to the Grand Ole Opry on radio, and he counted Bob Wills among his favorite musicians.

Merle Haggard became a country musician after a brief career of delinquency and crime and nearly three years in San Quentin. Bakersfield was, by the late 1950s, a country-music center of sorts. Buck Owens, who arrived from Texas by way of Arizona around 1950, made the city his headquarters; some wags called it "Buckersfield." Night clubs were plentiful, and there were opportunities to perform on radio. Haggard married Bonnie Owens, from Blanchard, Oklahoma, by way of (like her ex-husband Buck) Arizona. By the mid-1960s Haggard's career had assumed respectable proportions. He had made several recordings, but his release of 1969, "Okie from Muskogee," was the song that brought him national prominence.

Unhappily, "Okie from Muskogee" cast Haggard in the role of right-wing superpatriot, when, in fact, he held no political views and seldom even bothered to vote. The song was written on a bus—someone had seen a sign saying so-many-miles to Muskogee—and it required about twenty minutes to write, with time out for uncontrolled laughter. It doubtless found favor with many who were angered by the student unrest of the 1960s and the imagery of the Vietnam-era counterculture—Richard Nixon praised the song—but its popularity would obscure for years Haggard's better musical expressions of his Oklahoma heritage. In songs like "Mama Tried" and "Hungry Eyes" he recalled the trials and tribulations of the Oklahomans in California in a manner more somber, more literate, and more moving than anyone, including Woody Guthrie, had done before. Some, like Kris Kristofferson, called them folk songs, recognizing, perhaps, the ballad tradition that is rural Oklahoma's legacy.

Oklahoma country-and-western performers with a California connection included Jean Shepard, born in Pauls Valley in 1933; Wanda Jackson, born in Maud in 1937; and Dallas Frazier, born in Spiro in 1939. Shepard's family moved to Visalia in 1944, and Jackson and Frazier grew up around Bakersfield. Music was an important part of each one's childhood. Texan Hank Thompson, who would move to Oklahoma in 1953, boosted the careers of both Shepard and Jackson. He heard Shepard in California and helped her obtain a contract with Capitol Records; her "Dear John Letter" was a top release during the Korean War. Jackson, whose family had returned to Oklahoma in the mid-1940s, was singing in Oklahoma City when Thompson heard her in 1954 and engineered a Decca contract for her. Later she would write "Kicking Our Hearts Around" for Thompson, and it became one of his many hit recordings . . . .

Frazier's career owed much to singer Ferlin Husky; he won a talent contest, took a job with Husky's band, and obtained a recording contract with Capitol. In the 1950s, Frazier appeared in Cliffie Stone's "Hometown Jamboree" television program in Los Angeles, where he performed with other Oklahomans, including Molly Bee (née Beachboard), who was born in Oklahoma City in 1939 and who had lived for several years in Arizona . . . .

Doyle Holly, born in Oklahoma City in 1936, was for several years a member of Buck Owens's band, the Buckaroos . . . .

And Owens, who put Bakersfield on the musical map, had

Jean Shepard

worked as a studio musician in Hollywood in the mid-1950s, backing recording sessions for Wanda Jackson . . . .

It is not surprising that Oklahomans abroad in the land would have intersecting careers. There were some striking coincidences, to be sure—and we shall consider more of them—but they were to some extent to be expected, given the specialized nature of country-and-western music and that, until television introduced the music to large numbers of people in prime time during the 1960s, audiences remained white, with rural or working-class backgrounds. Performers tended to comprise a close-knit group, and stories abounded of assistance rendered to younger musicians by well-established country-music stars.

Hank Thompson's support of Jean Shepard and Wanda Jackson had many parallels. Ernest Tubb, the Texas Troubadour, helped Hank Snow, Hank Williams, and Johnny Cash obtain places on the Grand Ole Opry; but he also helped Cal Smith from Sallisaw, for years a member of Tubb's band and by the 1970s, owing to Tubb's encouragement, a star in his own right. Norma Jean Beasler, born in Wellston, went from local programs in Oklahoma City to national television exposure, thanks to the interest of Porter Wagoner, who asked her to join the cast of his syndicated show. And so forth.

Country music underwent changes in form and substance in the 1960s and 1970s. Live music all but disappeared from radio programming, and local music shows on television gave way to nationally syndicated programs. The record industry became more important as a means of introducing new talent—radio relied exclusively on recorded music, the culmination of a trend that began after World War II—and, as the industry grew, it began to exert pressure on performers. Vast sums of money were involved. Originally, record companies had tailored their products for specific audiences; the so-called race records of the 1920s and 1930s reflected that marketing policy—blues music for blacks, hillbilly music for rural whites, cajun music for the bayous of Louisiana, and so forth. These recordings were produced in relatively small numbers. But the proliferation of radio stations and, more importantly, home receiving sets in the late 1920s would begin a trend toward cultural homogenization that would make "race records" both impractical and unprofitable. Record companies sought to appeal to larger audiences, and radio was the medium of choice.

Largely as a result of economics, country music—or the country music heard on the radio—became more sophisticated. The hillbilly image was relegated to the Grand Ole Opry and confined to the South. The cowboy image, embraced by many musicians in the 1930s and 1940s as an alternative to the hayseed, bumpkin, and/or clodhopper characteristics of the hillbilly stereotype, persisted in the public performances of people like Porter Wagoner, but their songs came to present a harsher view of life. Wagoner, otherwise a cowboy, sang of alcoholism, adultery, and insanity, reflecting, one supposes, a more sophisticated perspective on American lifestyles in the 1960s. Traditional rural music was renamed "old time" music or reassigned to the category of "bluegrass," a label developed for the music of cultural conservatives like Bill Monroe, who steadfastly refused to change either the songs or the instrumentation and looked upon amplification as a technological aberration to be avoided at all costs. Some performers with long-established reputations could resist the pressures inherent in the music business. But many had to change or lapse into obscurity. The record that most companies and musicians wanted was something called a "crossover hit," a song ostensibly in the country-and-western genre but with appeal to other record buyers.

Country music contributed nearly as much to the development of rock and roll as black-oriented rhythm and blues did. Rockabilly music, combining the twelve-bar blues form with a

Oklahoma's country-music performers have been a conservative lot. The state has produced no exponent of "outlaw" music, unless one counts Hugo's Ray Wylie Hubbard, composer of "Redneck Mother," even though concerts by visiting Texans like Willie Nelson have been uniformly well attended. Only one—Cal Smith—made news by expressing a controversial political opinion, and that had to do with his support of the farmers' tractorcade to Washington, D.C., in the late 1970s, not with the workings of the Nashville music industry. Indeed, most Oklahoma-born performers have aligned themselves with Nashville and the Grand Ole Opry. Jean Shepard, a member of the Opry since 1955 and often an outspoken critic of the kinds of music some people seem willing to label "country," did protest the appearance of soul-singer James Brown at the Opry in March, 1979; she simply refused to share the stage with him, for no other reason than that he was not a country artist.

There have been other Oklahoma musicians who accepted no compromise with recording-industry trends. Lloyd ("Cowboy") Copas, born in Muskogee, in 1913, was one. An accomplished guitarist even as a child, Copas left Muskogee to pursue a career in music in 1929. He performed on radio stations throughout the Middle West, dividing time between Cincinnati and Knoxville. During World War II his recording of "Filipino Baby" was a hit for King Records, as were his "Tragic Romance" and "Signed, Sealed and Delivered." In 1946 he joined the Grand Ole Opry with Pee Wee King, and in the late 1940s he scored consecutive hits with "Tennessee Waltz," "Tennessee Moon," and "Candy Kisses." In the 1950s, however, his popularity faded. He did not change his style or his music, but rather he accepted small-town engagements and one-nighters, deciding simply to struggle through. In 1959 he negotiated a recording contract with Starday Records, and his 1960 hit "Alabam" took him again to the Opry and the top. In 1961 he re-released "Signed, Sealed and Delivered," and it was a hit again, nearly

Lloyd "Cowboy" Copas

twenty years after his first recording of it. Inasmuch as Starday was a purely country label, sold in outlets where customers looked for country music, Copas's newfound success was perhaps predictable; a small company in comparison to the Nashville giants like Capitol and RCA Victor, Starday was marketing its releases to a specific audience in a manner reminiscent of the old days of the "race records." Copas had demonstrated that there was an audience for his kind of music, and he had reached it with a small, specialized company at a time when the larger companies courted artists with wider appeal. But Copas did not reap the fruits of his persistent effort. He died in a plane crash with Patsy Cline and Jean Shepard's husband, Hawkshaw Hawkins, near Camden, Tennessee, in March, 1963.

The Willis Brothers made no compromise, either. Guy Willis was born in Arkansas in 1915, shortly before the family moved to Oklahoma. His brother Skeeter was born in Coalton in 1917. The family moved to Schulter, and there Vic was born in 1922. Like so many others we have mentioned, the brothers grew up in an environment rich in music. The Willises were a farm family, and the hard times of the 1930s led the brothers to seek work as musicians. In 1932 they found a job with radio station KGEF in Shawnee, and through the rest of the decade they appeared regularly on radio in Tulsa and Oklahoma City, as well as Gallup, New Mexico, and Kansas City.

The Willis Brothers were polished musicians. Guy played guitar and was the group's spokesman. Vic performed on accordian and piano, and Skeeter played the fiddle. They laced their repertoire with some of Guy's original compositions, and they developed the ability to imitate other country musicians. Versatility was a Willis Brothers hallmark, reflected in their work with Eddy Arnold and Hank Williams. Indeed, the Willis Brothers were the first group to back Williams, and at one point they even became Williams's "Drifting Cowboys." They served a brief stint with the Grand Ole Opry in the late 1940s, worked as studio musicians for many recording sessions, toured extensively, recorded for several labels, rejoined the Opry in 1960, and participated in USO tours through the 1960s.

In 1974 the Country Music Association chose Australian pop-singer Olivia Newton-John as female vocalist of the year. Objecting country artists formed the Association of Country Entertainers and, within two years, conducted a poll in fan magazines to determine audience preferences. The findings resulted in an ACE attack on radio-station playlists and programming practices. ACE Executive Director Vic Willis reported in 1977 that his organization would not release its membership list because some performers had been threatened with reprisals by radio stations angered by the ACE poll. The Willis Brothers had not changed in forty-five years, nor, they believed, had their audience; but the media had. They had the moral support of Jean Shepard, who claimed that radio stations were killing country music and that the Country Music Association awards were "not on the up-and-up."

Tommy Overstreet, born in Oklahoma City in 1934, seemed to be one artist in the 1970s who was concerned with identifying and adapting to trends. Reared in Texas, he was close to his cousin, Gene Austin, "the Bing Crosby of the 1920s" whose theme song was "My Blue Heaven." Overstreet took Austin as his role model, spending summers between semesters at the University of Texas on the road with the older man. Overstreet gained experience as a singer, a writer, and a record-company executive; and in 1970 his career as a country performer had begun. By 1977 he had enjoyed seventeen straight hits, five of which reached the top of the country-music charts. Many of his songs had a decidedly pop orientation. There is evidence also that Overstreet worried about a "non-descript" image, a concern that in the late 1970s led him to grow a beard and stop dyeing his gray hair, to dress more conservatively, and to

Tommy Overstreet

drop ABC Records in favor of the more forward-thinking Elektra label.

Oklahoma City's Henson Cargill enjoyed brief but phenomenal success in the country music field as a result of his hit of 1968, "Skip-a-Rope." Despite the half-dozen albums and more than thirty-five singles that followed that release, Cargill never had another hit, in part because he could not find the right song and in part because of his troubled relationships with record companies. He finally found the right song, something called "Silence on the Line," and he tried to resolve the recording dilemma by starting his own company in Oklahoma City—in his father's law offices, to be precise. Cargill had no desire to live in Nashville but preferred to remain in Oklahoma, working local dates. In the early 1980s his Copper Mountain Records was no nearer reestablishing his career than previous companies had been. Nevertheless, Cargill's name remained important in the history of country music because of "Skip-a-Rope," a song that in some ways violated industry taboos, inasmuch as it dealt realistically with the dissolution of family life and its effect on children.

The changes that have characterized the country-music business correspond to alterations in the public's perception of nearly every aspect of the entertainment industry. The countless hopefuls who head for Hollywood to break into motion pictures or for Florida to try out for the major leagues or for Nashville either to sell songs or to record them have all been seduced by the glamor of stardom and the attendant multi-digit salaries so frequently touted in the media. The complexities of the business are at first elusive, and while there are those whose lives testify to what may be achieved through relentless effort, one fact becomes patently obvious: there are more talented people than there are contracts, more potential stars than there are dollars to pay them, produce them, and promote them. The commercialization of music underscores the cultural changes that distinguish America in the twentieth century from America in the nineteenth, and the competent musician who might have achieved some local popularity a hundred years ago at sings and dances now must, at some point, accept both the realization that there are thousands of people around who are as good as he and the frustration of knowing that stardom will probably remain elusive. The intangible factors of public acceptance or just plain luck may affect musical careers, but those who have not achieved the fame (or the income) to which they aspire are secure in the knowledge that they have plenty of company. Indeed, organizations such as the Oklahoma Country Music Association provide a forum for established local performers, encourage new talent, and generally work toward a heightened professionalism among their membership through, among other things, monthly concerts and annual awards programs.

None of which is to suggest that Oklahoma has stopped producing headline country-and-western performers. That is hardly the case.

Big Al Downing, born in Centralia in 1941, grew up on a diet of Bob Wills and Hank Thompson, played on the radios of the truck drivers whose rigs he loaded as a young man. In the late 1950s he was Wanda Jackson's piano player, and by the mid-1970s he had reached the top of the record charts with a disco hit entitled "I'll Be Holdin' On," a curiosity inasmuch as its instrumentation featured a banjo. In 1978 he released "Mr. Jones" which climbed into the top twenty on country charts, making Downing the only other black performer since superstar Charley Pride to accomplish such a feat. It also made him the first Oklahoma black since Seminole's Stoney Edwards to gain national recognition as a country-and-western performer. His "The Story Behind the Story" and "Daddy Played the Banjo" were successful releases of 1980, although most Oklahoma radio stations that aired the songs seemed unaware that Downing was a local product.

Reba McEntire, born in Chockie and still an area resident, began recording for Mercury in 1976, with the help of Red Steagall. Married to rancher Charlie Battles, she lives near her father's 7,000-acre spread and has no desire to leave Oklahoma for Nashville or anywhere else. Her Mercury albums are quality productions, and from them have come a number of hit singles. Occasionally, McEntire has written her own material, but like Cal Smith and Tommy Overstreet she is building a career as a vocalist rather than as a composer.

Country-and-western music will continue to be an important element in Oklahoma's popular culture, simply because of the rural orientation of many of the state's inhabitants. Culturally, at least, the cosmopolitan pretensions of urban areas like Tulsa, Oklahoma City, and Lawton have had little impact on the listening habits of Oklahomans; and it is surely not without significance that Oklahoma's educational television network finds it financially advantageous to air Grand Ole Opry broadcasts and films of country-and-western television programs of the 1950s. The rural values that shaped much of Oklahoma's cultural heritage are no less important in the 1980s than they were in the 1880s, despite the substantial changes in the social and economic structure of the region in the intervening century.

Sources

The biographical sources cited for chapter 4 apply to this chapter as well. The statistical analyses of Richard A. Peterson and Russell Davis, Jr., are contained in their article, "The Fertile Crescent of Country Music," in *Journal of Country Music* 6, no. 1 (Spring 1975):19-27. Merle Haggard's career is discussed in Paul Hemphill, *The Good Old Boys* (New York: Simon and Schuster, 1974), chap. 9. Insights into country music on radio may be found in Richard A. Peterson and Marcus V. Gowan, "What's in a Country Music Band Name," *Journal of Country Music* 2, no. 4 (Winter 1971):

pp. 1-9. Information on Tommy Overstreet, Cal Smith, Jean Shepard, and the Association of Country Entertainers may be found in various news stories by Associated Press writer Joe Edwards, filed between 1977 and 1979. Henson Cargill's career is discussed in Covey Bean, "Huntin' for a Country Hit," *The Oklahomans (Sunday Oklahoman)*, March 9, 1980, pp. 4-6, and for the early history of the Oklahoma Country Music Association see Jeff Holladay, "Now Country's Made in Oklahoma," *Orbit Magazine (Sunday Oklahoman)*, August 31, 1975, pp. 9-12, 14-15. The careers of Big Al Downing and Reba McEntire are reported by Bob Allen in *Country Music*, January-February 1980, pp. 19-20, 24, 26.

The following recordings are representative: Elton Britt, *The Wandering Cowboy* (ABC-Paramount ABC-293) and *Something for Everyone* (ABC Paramount ABC-566); Merle Haggard, *Okie from Muskogee* (Capital ST-384), recorded in concert in Muskogee; *Jean Shepard's Greatest Hits* (United Artists UA-LA 685-G); Wanda Jackson, *There's a Party Goin' On* (Capitol T-1511), and for contrast, *Now I Have Everything* (Myrrh MST-6533), an album released after her spiritual rebirth and her announcement to abandon secular music, notable for the cut entitled "Jesus Put a Yodel in My Soul"; *The Best of Hank Thompson* (Capitol SM-1878); Cal Smith, *Country Bumpkin* (MCA-424), *My Kind of Country* (MCA-485), and *The Best of Cal Smith* (MCA-70); Cowboy Copas, *Shake a Hand* (Starday SLP 371) and *The Best of Cowboy Copas* (Starday SLP 948); *The Best of the Willis Brothers* (Starday SLP 466); Tommy Overstreet, *Better Me* (ABC AY-1066) and *The Real Tommy Overstreet* (Elektra GE-226); Big Al Downing, "The Story Behind the Story" (Warner Bros. WBS 49161); Stoney Edwards, *Mississippi You're on My Mind* (Capitol St-11401); Reba McEntire, *Out of a Dream* (Mercury SRM-1-5017) and *Feel the Fire* (Mercury SRM-1-5029); and, for the Collins Kids, *Rockabilly Stars*, vol. 2 (Epic EG 37621), which contains five of their songs, and *Rockin' Rollin' Collins Kids* (Bear Family BFX 15074), an album of previously unreleased recordings made from 1955 to 1958 (Bear Family is a West German label).

Peter Guralnick, *Lost Highway: Journeys and Arrivals of American Musicians* (Boston: D. R. Godine, 1979), contains insightful chapters on Merle Haggard and Stoney Edwards and is useful for an understanding of the rockabilly phenomenon.

Of the Willis Brothers, Skeeter is dead and Guy has retired. Vic Willis continues to record with the Vic Willis Trio.

8. The Oklahoma All-Stars

AS a largely rural and predominantly white state, Oklahoma might have been expected to produce large numbers of country-and-western musicians. Indeed, the rural context of Oklahoma's popular culture, personified nationally by people like Will Rogers or Gene Autry, might suggest that the jazz of the Oklahoma City Blue Devils and Charlie Christian was an anomalous development, atypical artistically, and nothing more — or less — than a phase through which musically inclined Oklahomans passed on their way to somewhere else. But the facts are that Oklahoma produced many more prominent jazz musicians than it did any other kind, and that its contributions to the jazz mainstream have been more extensive and of greater consequence than any to other aspects of American culture. The Blue Devils were only a beginning.

In the decades between the Depression and the Vietnam War, Oklahoma jazz musicians were everywhere on the national and international jazz scene. Their careers intersected and in many cases influenced profoundly the music of people whose names were perhaps better known. The example of Charlie Parker is instructive in this regard.

Charlie Parker was the "Bird," from the nickname "Yardbird," signifying a chicken, a cognomen awarded by associates remarking on his predilection for the fried form of that fowl. He was a premier alto saxophonist and authentic jazz genius, and virtually everything he ever recorded is still available today, so central is he to the history of American jazz. Through cascading sixteenth notes, he spoke musically "like a consumer of basic English," said Leonard Feather, "who had suddenly swallowed the whole dictionary yet miraculously managed to digest every page" to help "create a new language for jazz."

Parker was born in Kansas City, Kansas, in 1920. He grew up in Kansas City, Missouri, listening as a teenager to the music of saxophonist Lester Young, formerly with the Blue Devils and by the late 1930s making his first recordings with Count Basie's Orchestra. When Parker acquired an instrument of his own, he bought Young's records and copied his solos. He studied for a time with another saxophonist, Buster Smith, who had moved to Kansas City after leaving the Blue Devils. A boy without a father, Parker called Smith "Dad" and learned a great deal about music from him.

Parker spent some time in New York but returned to Kansas City in 1939, and there he was recruited by pianist Jay McShann for a new band he was forming. McShann had been born and reared in Muskogee.

Charlie Parker was, according to musicologist James Lincoln Collier, a sociopath: he did not like people very much, and his vices did not help. Parker drank and used narcotics, especially heroin. McShann did not care for his excesses—high or straight, tight or sober, Parker was both a glutton and a womanizer—and Parker did not appreciate McShann's discipline or what he considered to be McShann's musical conservatism. Yet it was under McShann's tutelage that Parker began to develop his style and to learn to be a professional.

Parker left McShann's group in mid-1942, spent three more

years in New York, and went to California in 1946. In Los Angeles he played some concerts with Lester Young, the paragon become peer. The excesses continued, and heroin landed Parker in Camarillo State Hospital, where he remained for seven months. (Indeed, Parker's lifestyle would have killed a lesser man a good deal quicker than it killed Parker. He died in 1955 at the age of 34. The doctor who prepared the death certificate did not know his age, but surveyed the remains and made an estimate: he wrote that Charlie Parker was 53.)

Camarillo released the Bird early in 1947, and friends arranged some recording sessions. The last one, his California farewell, was held in Hollywood on February 26, and it produced "Relaxin' at Camarillo," "Cheers," "Carvin' the Bird," and "Stupendous," which rank among Parker's best recordings. He performed that day with a group of musicians identified on subsequent record labels as the Charlie Parker All Stars. And all-stars they were: pianist Dodo Marmarosa and bassist George ("Red") Callender had backed Lester Young; trumpet player Howard McGhee had worked with Lionel Hampton, Andy Kirk, Charlie Barnet, Basie, and Coleman Hawkins; tenor-saxophonist 'Vardell Gray was an Earl Hines alumnus who would go on to Basie and Benny Goodman; drummer Don Lamond was fresh from Woody Herman's orchestra; and the guitarist was Barney Kessel, then a Ben Pollack and Charlie Barnet veteran. Kessel, as we have seen, was a Muskogee native. Wardell Gray and Don Lamond were born in Oklahoma City. Howard McGhee was from Tulsa. And Charlie Parker was never that good again.

Jay McShann was born in Muskogee in 1909 and first learned about music from an older sister. The McShann family (Jay had three sisters) was unable to pay for more than one series of lessons, but one sister was sent to study piano with a local teacher, a Mrs. Bell, whose son, Samuel Aaron Bell, would eventually teach music in a Muskogee high school, acquire a

Jay McShann

Master's degree from New York University, and become the bassist for the Duke Ellington Orchestra.[1] Jay McShann learned secondhand, by listening and by watching his sister practice, but with one important difference: he did not bother to learn to read music. He was twelve years old then. Later, he learned to play the organ by following the same procedure, and when he played for church services he had to remind himself to open the hymnal to the appropriate selection so that the worshippers would think he was doing it properly. He listened to a great deal of popular music, on records, on radio, and as performed by visiting bands, like Bennie Moten's group. He would remember the local performances of a band led by Clarence Love as the musical catalyst that made him want to play jazz.

McShann completed high school in Muskogee and briefly attended Nashville's Fisk University. He still could not read music. He returned to Muskogee, a restless teenager who found small-town existence now dull, and, with his father's backing, he went to Tulsa, literally to seek his fortune. He found Al Denny's band, a group without a piano player. He stood outside the rehearsal hall until he had memorized some of Denny's tunes, and then he offered himself for an audition. He won the job, his hands roaming the keyboard, his eyes fixed upon arrangements he could not read. The other musicians were tremendously excited: here was a kid who had walked in off the street and could sight-read their scores and improvise as well! But McShann's was not a long-lived deception. The truth became apparent as soon as they hit something he had never heard and therefore had not memorized. They were disappointed, but the boy had

[1] Bell earned a doctorate at Columbia University in 1977. As chairman of the Department of Performing Arts, in Essex County College, Newark, New Jersey, he lectured extensively on Ellington's music and influence and composed music of his own, notably "Bicentennial Symphony—A Jazz Composition."

ability; they kept him on, and they worked to teach him what he needed to know.

McShann's subsequent peregrinations were typical of the professional musician. He spent some time in Arkansas as the leader of a small band and then went back to college for a year in Kansas. Broke and reduced to swiping food from his landlady, he left Kansas for Oklahoma City, where he found a job with Eddie Hall and His Bostonians, a band headquartered in Shawnee. He toured Arizona and New Mexico with Hill, but the group dissolved in 1934.

McShann had discovered Kansas City on a trip north to visit relatives in Iowa, and by 1935 he was working regularly in clubs there. As we saw in chapter 3, Kansas City musicians could ignore the Depression; and McShann liked the environment well enough to remain (with a few months off for work in Chicago) until late 1940, by which time he was leading his own orchestra—the one in which Charlie Parker performed. He took that group to New York, where it was warmly received by jazz audiences. After a year of military service, he reestablished the band in New York in 1945 and divided his time between the coasts during the rest of the decade. He was most closely associated with the Kansas City musical scene, however, and he returned to it in the early 1950s, remaining for nearly two decades. During the 1970s he toured in Canada and Europe, often in company with fellow Muskogee-native Claude Williams, jazz violinist and formerly guitarist for the Basie orchestra.

Known in later years primarily as a club performer, McShann enjoyed renewed popularity in the late 1970s as a result of Bruce Ricker's documentary film, *The Last of the Blue Devils*, a study of Kansas City music that took as its point of departure the old Oklahoma City commonwealth band and focused on the recollections of alumni like Basie and Buster Smith. McShann figured in the film as an exponent of what Ricker described as the distinctive Kansas City jazz style, and, as the film continued to garner the accolades of music and cinema critics alike, he was billed with Basie and Joe Turner as one of the documentary's "stars." Announcements of subsequent club appearances —and even a record album—proclaimed McShann to be the "last" Blue Devil. McShann, of course, had never been a member of the Oklahoma City band, and the label both annoyed and embarrassed him. At the age of seventy, however, he was still going strong as a result of the film and was resurrecting the big band sound in his recorded work.

It is remarkable that Jay McShann, Claude Williams, Samuel Aaron Bell, and Barney Kessel all were born in Muskogee. Theirs are names sufficiently prominent to secure that community's place in the history of American jazz, but they were not the only musicians the town produced. There were the Thomas brothers, Walter (born in 1907) and Joseph (born in 1908), who were tenor saxophonists with Jelly Roll Morton's band in the late 1920s. Walter, nicknamed "Foots," left Morton for a thirteen-year stint in Cab Calloway's reed section, doubling on clarinet and flute and doing some arranging. He led his own group in New York in the mid-1940s, retiring as a professional musician in 1948 to become a talent manager and booking agent; he was also involved in a music-publishing company with drummer Cozy Cole. Joe Thomas went on to become an "artists and repertoire" executive with Decca Records and RCA Victor.

And there was Don Byas, born Carlos Wesley Byas in Muskogee in 1912, a tenor saxophonist who worked at various times with Basie, Coleman Hawkins, Dizzy Gillespie, and Ellington. Byas began as a violin student but switched to alto saxophone and performed as a teenager with people like Bennie Moten. He was a member of the Oklahoma City Blue Devils in the late 1920s before attending Langston University and forming his own band there, a group known as Don Carlos and His Collegiate Ramblers (from whence came the "Don" by which he was

95

Don Byas

known thereafter). He switched to tenor saxophone in 1933 and worked through the decade with a number of bands, including Buck Clayton's and Andy Kirk's.

Byas joined the Count Basie Orchestra in 1941, replacing Lester Young, who had gone to California to start his own group. He stayed with Basie until 1943 and spent the mid-1940s on 52nd Street in New York with Dizzy Gillespie and others, and leading his own band. The transition from the swing music of the 1930s to the "bop" of the 1940s was not an easy one for many performers to make, but Byas was a musician who had no trouble. He had received valuable exposure with Basie and had made some splendid recordings, but the mid-1940s was the period of his greatest popularity. In 1946 he toured Europe with Don Redman's band and became the first of a number of prominent American jazz expatriates. European audiences seemed more appreciative than American ones, more enthusiastic, and less inclined to criticize innovation. He returned to the United States briefly in 1970 to appear at the Newport Jazz Festival, but by then he was virtually unknown in his own country. He died of lung cancer in Amsterdam in 1972, but as late as 1979 recordings of his European performances were still being issued in the United States.

Indeed, the entire northeastern quadrant of Oklahoma, of which Muskogee is a part, was a particularly fertile area for the production of jazz musicians. Sapulpa's Marshall Royal we have discussed in connection with the Basie Orchestra; and we have mentioned Howard McGhee, born in Tulsa in 1918, a veteran of several groups who toured both Europe and the Orient and who, in the 1970s, formed his own big band when other musicians wagered that the feat could not be accomplished in those inflationary and sophisticated times when small combos seemed to be the only practical way to play jazz. But northeastern Oklahoma also produced such notables as Chet Baker, Claude

Jones, John Jacob Simmons, Oscar Pettiford, and Lee Wiley. Baker, Pettiford, and Wiley would figure in anyone's history of American jazz as virtuoso performers, and Jones and Simmons were two of the idiom's better-known sidemen.

Claude Jones was born in Boley in 1901 and by 1914 was playing trombone in the town band. In high school in Langston he also played trumpet and drums. He attended Ohio's Wilberforce University and was pursuing a law degree there when he left in 1922 to join the band that became McKinney's Cotton Pickers. Jones remained with this group until 1929, and during the 1930s he worked with Fletcher Henderson's band, with Don Redman, with Chick Webb, and, from 1934 to 1940, with Cab Calloway. He also recorded on Jelly Roll Morton's last sessions for RCA Victor in 1939. He performed with several groups in the 1940s and is perhaps best remembered for his stint with the Ellington Orchestra from 1944 to 1948. In the early 1950s, with the demise of many of the big bands, Jones abandoned his musical career and became a steward on the liner S.S. *United States,* a job that he held until his death at sea in 1962. Principally a trombonist, Jones was occasionally featured as a vocalist with Ellington.

Born in Haskell in 1918, John Jacob Simmons was educated in Tulsa before moving to California during the Depression. Originally a trumpet player, he switched to string bass after an athletic injury and by 1940 had worked as bassist for such musicians as Nat ("King") Cole (then better known as a jazz pianist than as a vocalist) and Roy Eldridge. In the 1940s he performed with Benny Goodman, Louis Armstrong, Duke Ellington, and Illinois Jacquet, did freelance studio work, and joined the Columbia Broadcasting System studio orchestra. He played for two years with Errol Garner in the early 1950s, but by middecade he was relatively inactive, and he did not perform much after about 1960.

Chet Baker was born Chesney H. Baker in Yale, Oklahoma,

Chet Baker

in 1929, two months after the Wall Street crash. His father was a country-and-western guitarist, but Baker received no formal musical training until 1940 when the family migrated to California. He played trumpet in high school and during two Army enlistments (1946-48 and 1950-52), and he studied music briefly in El Camino Junior College, in Torrance, California, shortly after it opened its doors in 1949. He performed with Charlie Parker in 1952, the year in which he gained wide recognition for his solo on the Gerry Mulligan Quartet's recording of "My Funny Valentine." Beginning in 1953, Baker won jazz polls sponsored by *Down Beat* and *Metronome* magazines, *Playboy,* and various European publications, both as an instrumentalist and as a vocalist. Doug Ramsey, noting that among fans and critics Baker was more popular on trumpet than Dizzy Gillespie, Louis Armstrong, and Miles Davis and was at least as popular as Nat Cole as a vocalist, has suggested that the success and the fame were too much for the soft-spoken young man from Oklahoma. Or perhaps the temptations of the professional musician's life were too great. In any case, Baker was a heroin addict by 1957 and would possibly have succumbed as Charlie Parker had, if five other addicts had not rolled him one night in San Francisco in 1968, beating him to a pulp in the process and extracting his teeth for good measure. Having narrowly escaped death, Baker entered a methadone treatment program and recovered his health. He did not play the trumpet for two years, in part because of the damage to his mouth; indeed, he had to relearn the instrument, no simple matter, as he observed, for a toothless person. He struggled back and by 1973 was performing and recording again, recovering his reputation and his position as a premier instrumentalist.

Oscar Pettiford was born in Okmulgee in 1922, into the enormous family of veterinarian "Doc" Pettiford. His mother was a music teacher, and the Pettiford children evidenced early talents and abilities. Oscar Pettiford began playing piano at the age of

Oscar Pettiford

eleven and learned the string bass at age fourteen. His parents formed a family band with Pettiford and ten of his siblings, and the group toured the country to appreciative audiences in the 1930s. Pettiford joined Charlie Barnet in the early 1940s and by 1943 was a regular in New York, performing at Minton's and along 52nd Street with Roy Eldridge and Dizzy Gillespie. In the late 1940s he worked with Coleman Hawkins and Woody Herman and spent two years in Duke Ellington's orchestra. In the 1950s he was a free-lance musician, toured the Orient with his own band (which included Howard McGhee), and did session work in New York. In 1958 he went to Great Britain on a concert tour and decided to remain in Europe, like Don Byas another Oklahoma expatriate. By then, Pettiford had begun playing jazz on the violoncello while maintaining his reputation as an outstanding bassist. Dizzy Gillespie said that he was an authentic jazz genius, a remark with which few who heard Pettiford would disagree. Gillespie also noted that the Oklahoman was "a driving force" in the development of bebop—and here we may recall Charlie Christian's contributions as well. When Oscar Pettiford died in 1960, he had made his permanent home in Denmark.

Lee Wiley was born in Fort Gibson in 1915, and in 1930 she ran away from home. By 1932 she was a well-known vocalist in New York and Chicago jazz clubs and on radio. During the Depression era she was noted as a pop singer, principally because of her radio performances. She shared "The Pond's Program" with Eleanor Roosevelt and worked with Paul Whiteman and Victor Young. She joined Eddie Condon's group in 1939 and in the mid-1940s toured with pianist Jess Stacy's band (they were married for five years). She recorded through the 1950s and 1960s, occasionally performing in concerts or on television. In August, 1975, she announced plans to make still another album, but within four months she was dead. When they buried her in Fort Gibson, hardly anyone noticed, even though the critics had labeled her a truly distinctive vocalist and jazz fans treasured her old recordings and both agreed upon her importance. Her appeal, they said, was that of a small-town girl from Oklahoma, the charming teenager of Cherokee ancestry who sang so delicately, so sweetly.

They all might as well have been expatriates. To read about them—but not in state histories—is to ask, Is there *any* jazz musician beloved or bragged upon by Oklahomans? In 1977, Chet Baker released an album that suggests the experience of so many: *You Can't Go Home Again.*

And yet, there were so many who might have come home again, so many who could have. It is more than a little ironic that a state which has contributed so much to the history of American jazz is also a state that nowadays provides no forum for jazz musicians and takes no note of its musical native sons and daughters. In some cases, there is perhaps the unhappy notoriety of a heroin-addicted Chet Baker or a marijuana-smoking Charlie Christian that prevents local recognition: Wardell Gray, born in Oklahoma City in 1921, influenced by the music of Lester Young, and a participant in those Charlie Parker sessions, died of an overdose of narcotics (some say he was murdered) in Las Vegas in 1955; but you will rarely hear a better tenor saxophonist. In some cases, there is perhaps a problem with the music, at least for some listeners: Don Cherry, born in Oklahoma City in 1936, is most often remembered for his work with saxophonist Ornette Coleman, whose career seemed dedicated to pushing jazz music beyond the limits imposed by melody or tempo or instrumentation or even the endurance of his musicians; but Don Cherry is still there, in the vanguard of modern jazz, experimenting with exotic scales and diverse musical forms and issuing records at an astonishing rate.

And if one does not recall Lee Wiley, one is not likely to remember the other vocalists: Kay Starr, born Kathryn Starks in Dougherty in 1922, who sang with Glenn Miller, Bob Crosby, Joe Venuti, and Charlie Barnet; or Lea Mathews, born in Mc-

103

Alester in 1925, who toured with Woody Herman; or Marilyn Moore, born in Oklahoma City in 1931, who sang with Barnet and Herman and who, according to the critics, sounded a great deal like Billie Holiday.

The list, of course, seems endless: trombonist Moe Schneider, born in Bessie in 1919, whose music may be caught on the late show in jazz films of the 1950s like *Pete Kelly's Blues, The Gene Krupa Story,* or *The Five Pennies;* pianist Stan Wrights-man, born in Oklahoma City in 1910, who went from local bands to the soundtrack of William Holden's film, *Picnic,* and television series like *M-Squad* and *Bourbon Street Beat;* pianist Howard Smith, born in Ardmore in 1910, who toured with Benny Goodman, Red Norvo, Glenn Miller, and Tommy Dorsey in the 1930s and was Dorsey's pianist on "Boogie Woogie" before becoming a studio musician in 1940; et cetera.

In discussing jazz music and its relationship to the cultural history of Oklahoma, it is a simple matter to belabor the point: this is the history that few people know, despite the abundance of its sources. There are books yet to be written on the subject: that northeastern quadrant deserves study; Muskogee alone would make for a fascinating investigation. But this volume is intended merely as an introduction, and, as I have said, the point is easy to belabor. That this is only a prelude is suggested by the listings in such biographical directories as Chilton's *Who's Who of Jazz:* Buddy Anderson, Abe Bolar, Henry Bridges, Elmer E. Crumbley, Theodore Donnelly, George James, Lem Johnson, Orlando Robeson, Francis Whitby . . . , Oklahomans all, whether the state acknowledges them or not.

Sources

In addition to the biographical sources listed for chapter 3, see James Lincoln Collier, *The Making of Jazz: A Comprehensive History* (Boston: Houghton Mifflin Co., 1978), especially pp. 362-76. Leonard Feather's remarks on Charlie Parker are from *The Book of Jazz: From Then Till Now*, p. 110. For Jay McShann, see Stanley Dance, *The World of Count Basie*, pp. 249-51. For detailed overview of Bruce Ricker's film, see John Fell, "Last of the Blue Devils," *Film Quarterly* 24 (Winter 1980-81):53-56.

The Charlie Parker All Stars are heard on *The Very Best of Bird* (Warner Bros. 2 WB 3198).

Jay McShann's *Early Bird* (Spotlite SPJ 120) features the 1940s orchestra with Charlie Parker. Other useful McShann albums include *The Man from Muskogee* (Sackville 3005), a Canadian release featuring Claude Williams; *The Last of the Blue Devils* (Atlantic SD 8800), which is a fine example of the Kansas City sound; and *The Big Apple Bash* (Atlantic SD 8804), a McShann reconstruction of the big band era.

The Walter "Foots" Thomas All Stars (Prestige 7584) features Thomas instrumentally and contains several of his compositions. Thomas died in 1981. Don Byas's work may be heard on *Savoy Jam Party* (Savoy 2213), a two-record set, and *A Tribute to Cannonball* (Columbia JC 35755), a recent issue of a European session with pianist Bud Powell. Samuel Aaron Bell is featured on Johnny Hodges, *The Smooth One* (Verve VE-2-2532) and Duke Ellington, *Unknown Session* (Columbia JC 35342).

Howard McGhee appears on Andy Kirk and His Clouds of Joy, *Instrumentally Speaking, 1936-1942* (MCA-1308), and, with his 1960s big band, on *Cookin' Time* (Zim ZMS-2004). Claude Jones performs on Fletcher Henderson, *Swing's the Thing, 1931-34* (MCA-1318), and *The World of Duke Ellington* (Columbia CG 32564).

Chet Baker's *She Was Too Good to Me* (CTI 6050 S1) and *You Can't Go Home Again* (A&M SP 726) date from 1974 and 1977 respectively and mark Baker's return to jazz following his recovery from heroin addiction. *Broken Wing* (Inner City IC 1120) is a fine release of 1981. For a recent interview, see Maggie Hawthorn, "Chet Baker," *Down Beat*, October 1981, pp. 24-27, 63.

The Oscar Pettiford Memorial Album (Prestige 7813) is a good introduction to the Okmulgee bassist's work. His performances on *The World of Duke Ellington* (Columbia CG 32564) date from the late 1940s, while *My Little Cello* (Fantasy 6010) proceeded from his European experience in the late 1950s. Pettiford's sessions with pianist Thelonious Monk, reissued as *Brilliance* (Milestone M-47023), are well worth hearing.

Lee Wiley "On the Air" (Totem 1021) consists of her selected radio broadcasts of the 1930s, and she has two songs on *Jess Stacy's J. Stacy & Friends* (Commodore XFL 15358). She and Kay Starr appear on *Singin' the Blues: A Treasury of Great Jazz Singers of the 1930s, '40s and '50s* (MCA 2-4064), with several other Oklahoma musicians. Starr's *Movin'* (Capitol SM-1180) and *Just Plain Country* (Capitol SM-1795) suggest both her antecedents and her versatility.

The Wardell Gray Memorial Album (Prestige 7343) is a two-disc album containing some of Gray's best work. An unusual session of his with Dexter Gordon is available on *The Chase and the Steeple Chase* (MCA-1336). Don Cherry's efforts with Ornette Coleman may be heard on *Science Fiction* (Columbia KC 21061). *Don Cherry* (A&M SP 717) is a prime example of his exotica, as, to a lesser extent, are *Codona* (ECM-1-1132) and *Codona 2* (ECM-1-1177). Cherry's *Old and New Dreams* (ECM-1-1154) represents the best of his recent work.

Anthologies such as *Singin' the Blues,* listed above, often contain unexpected rewards in the form of material unavailable elsewhere. *Stars of the Apollo* (Columbia CG 30788), for example, offers Claude Jones, Hot Lips Page, Walter Page, Charlie Christian, Jimmy Rushing, Ed Lewis, Count Basie, Oscar Pettiford, and Jack Teagarden, all jazz musicians with an Oklahoma connection. *Leonard Feather Presents Encyclopedia of Jazz/ Vol. 3— The Forties, Vol. 4— The Fifties* (MCA 2-4062) includes Pettiford, Jay McShann, Pee Wee Russell (who studied clarinet in Muskogee) Don Byas, John Jacob Simmons, and Marshall Royal. The Time-Life Records *Giants of Jazz* series of three-disc sets is a gold mine of otherwise unavailable recordings, especially for anyone seeking examples of the work of Oklahoma sidemen, for example, Claude Jones on *Duke Ellington* (STL-J02). There is also a Pee Wee Russell set (STL-J17) in the series.

9. Rocking and Rolling

CONTRARY to the dictates of nostalgia, rock-and-roll music did not spring full-grown from the heads of Elvis Presley or the Beatles. Rather, it evolved, like every other musical form, from something else. Before rock and roll there was rhythm and blues, a commercial and urbanized form of rural folk blues, generally based on a twelve-bar structure with, where lyrics were involved, an AAB rhyme scheme. In its early manifestations, it was characterized by a heavy beat and lots of brass and reeds, and whether the tempo was fast or slow, it was the kind of music that was good for dancing—the jitterbug of the 1940s would give rise to all sorts of gyrations. The form was rural—blacks who favored blues music had migrated to cities in large numbers during World War II—but the instrumentation was urban, which eventually ·meant electric, and one could isolate a variety of elements: a bit of Benny Goodman's swing, the harmony saxophone sections characteristic of Foots Thomas's compositions, the Basie beat, the stride piano, the Kansas City blues shout. The suggestion of complexity in all of that is surely misleading. It was a simple music, based on a three-chord progression, difficult only for pianists or bassists or guitarists who had to play in B-flat so that the horns could operate in concert C, and that a consideration only for rank amateurs.

And the interesting point is that, initially, few rank amateurs were involved. Simpler the music may have been, but the musicians who were first attracted to rhythm and blues were jazz performers, trained and experienced people who made the transition because there was money in it. Rhythm and blues was popular with youngsters, and musicians who played it could find more frequent employment than they could by confining themselves to the jazz idiom for older and smaller audiences. There was also the growth and diversification of the record business in post-World War II America to consider. Rhythm and blues was music that appealed on any of several levels: it was basic, sometimes visceral, music, good for dancing; some rhythm-and-blues songs, like Louis Jordan's "Open the Door, Richard," were popular as novelty tunes; and some of the songs were laden with sexual innuendo and double entendre. Unlike jazz, rhythm and blues was not cerebral, and it did not present the listener with instrumental techniques, stylistic changes, or shifts of key and tempo for appreciation or debate. In short, it was a music of fewer nuances. Jazz performers found it lucrative—it would become increasingly so—and, in view of their backgrounds, ridiculously easy to play.

Earl Bostic was born in Tulsa in 1913 and studied clarinet and alto saxophone in high school there. He worked for three years with local bands before moving to New Orleans to attend Xavier University. In college he studied theory, harmony, and composition and learned to play several different instruments well, useful preparation for the nomadic existence he would lead in the 1930s, working with jazz bands in Louisiana, Ohio, and New York in the space of four years. By 1939 he had his own group—indeed, he seemed to be his own group, playing, in addition to alto sax, the trumpet, the guitar, and baritone

Earl Bostic

saxophone. In the early 1940s he performed with Hot Lips Page and as a member of Lionel Hampton's orchestra; and he arranged musical scores for Page, Louis Prima, Paul Whiteman, and Artie Shaw. In 1945 he obtained a contract with King Records, newly founded by an ex-haberdasher named Syd Nathan in an abandoned icehouse near Cincinnati. Nathan signed all sorts of artists for his label, including country-and-western performers (he would eventually sign Cowboy Copas), but rhythm-and-blues music was a major aspect of his enterprise: nearly every big-name urban-blues performer in the 1940s and 1950s would record for King.

Earl Bostic's association with King lasted twenty years, ending only with his death in 1965. King released three Bostic recordings in 1945 and issued new discs regularly thereafter, for pop audiences and the jukebox trade. His recording of "Flamingo" spent twenty weeks at the top of rhythm-and-blues charts in 1951 and remained his biggest hit. Singles and albums (more than a dozen for King alone) brought Bostic great popularity in the 1950s, when white teenagers were beginning to discover black music; but Bostic seems to have recorded whatever he pleased, leaving the determination of what was salable and what was not to record executives. (He was still playing jazz, too. In 1952 he hired saxophonist John Coltrane for his band, and by all accounts he taught Coltrane a great deal.) King's vaults overflowed with Bostic masters, and that they contained something for every occasion was demonstrated during the "bossa nova" craze in the early 1960s, when King's management found unreleased Bostic cuts that matched the bossa-nova tempo and issued them to capitalize on the Brazilian music's currency. Most of Bostic's material was recorded before 1956, when he had a massive heart attack; he did not perform again until 1959, and even then he remained in semiretirement. Even a dozen years after his death, the King vaults were still the source of new Bostic releases.

Other Oklahoma jazz musicians important in the history of rhythm and blues were Joe Liggins, a pianist and bandleader born in Guthrie in 1915, and Hal Singer, a tenor saxophonist born in Tulsa in 1919. Both men's music foreshadowed rock and roll.

Liggins's family moved to California in 1930, and in high school in San Diego he played the trumpet. He played it in Los Angeles as well, but perhaps a bit too enthusiastically: he had a stroke and had to give up the instrument for the piano. He formed a band and played rhythm and blues in the early 1940s, winning a contract with a new company, Exclusive Records, for which he and his group recorded two Liggins instrumental compositions, "The Honeydripper" and "I've Got a Right to Cry." The band quickly became known as Joe Liggins and His Honeydrippers, their careers were assured, and Exclusive became the dominant independent rhythm-and-blues label in the United States. That was because "The Honeydripper" (the term signifies a virile male in the patois of the street) sold more than a million copies during 1945-46, a level of sales never before achieved in rhythm-and-blues music.

In Chicago, record buyers stood in lines that were blocks long to obtain "The Honeydripper." Copies were in short supply in the midwest, and Pullman porters, knowing this, would purchase discs in California, carry them on trains to Chicago, and sell them to rhythm-and-blues fans for ten dollars apiece. Restaurant owners complained about the tune, demanding that it be removed from their jukeboxes: customers played it repeatedly, and waitresses were, according to Leon René, "reacting too strongly to the infectious beat and were hopping all over the place."

Hal Singer began playing the violin in Tulsa at the age of eight. He learned clarinet and tenor saxophone in high school before pursuing a degree in agriculture at Virginia's Hampton Institute. He became a professional musician and performed on

111

summer vacations during his college years with bands in central Oklahoma. He worked with several groups in the late 1930s and spent two years in Kansas City before joining Jay McShann in 1941. Between 1942 and 1947 he worked with several other Oklahoma musicians, including Don Byas and Hot Lips Page. He joined Duke Ellington in 1948 and then left him to make a rhythm-and-blues recording.

The song was "Cornbread," an instrumental, and Savoy Records released it in 1948. It became a hit, and Hal Singer became Cornbread Singer. On the strength of the record he acquired the capital to put together his own band and tour the country for a decade, making the transition from rhythm and blues to rock and roll. He performed in New York after 1958 and moved to France in 1965.

Lowell Fulson's musical experiences emphasize anew the notion of Oklahoma as a cultural melting pot. Fulson (sometimes spelled Fulsom) was born in Tulsa in 1921, of black and Indian ancestry, a descendant of Choctaw freedmen. In 1926, when his father died, Fulson's mother left the city for his grandfather's place in southeastern Oklahoma, between Wapanucka and Atoka; Fulson grew up there, attending a mission school, singing hymns in the Methodist church, and listening to his grandfather's violin and his uncles' guitars.

A twelve-year-old Lowell Fulson learned to sing country-and-western songs from a white musician named Coot Mason, who had performed with Jimmie Rodgers, the venerable father of commercial country music. Fulson also listened to records and learned the music of blues singers like Blind Boy Fuller and Blind Lemon Jefferson. He learned to play the guitar and backed into his first job at the age of thirteen: his cousin was in a band and on one occasion got too drunk to play at a local dance, so the other musicians asked Fulson to substitute.

Fulson performed in churches and at picnics, on a guitar that he bought in a pawn shop for half of his weekly wages—three dollars. In 1938 he moved to Ada and began playing in white clubs there, building a repertoire based on what customers requested. He was a part-Indian blues singer performing "Sail Along, Silvery Moon" and "Beer-Barrel Polka" for white patrons, and if that experience defies cultural analysis, so does his stint as a member of Dan Wright's twelve-piece string band that played Dixieland and bluegrass music and featured a one-armed, one-legged guitarist!

Fulson left Wright's band in 1939, shortly after he married. His wife was jealous of Wright's female pianist and frequently disrupted the group's performances, so Fulson confined his musical activities to Ada's Holiness Church and to singing in the cotton fields where he then earned a living. He disliked field work and began playing for tips in roadhouses. In one of these he met bluesman Texas Alexander and left with him for a year of travel in western Oklahoma and Texas. He returned to Ada, abandoned music for his wife's sake yet again, and moved with her to Texas, where he worked as a short-order cook in a bus station until he was drafted for military service in 1943. He spent two years in the navy in southern California, learning something about the rhythm-and-blues scene in Oakland and San Diego by performing in clubs when he could. Then, in 1945, he acquired an electric guitar and was sent to Guam for the duration. He was discharged in Norman in 1946 and found a job as a cook in Duncan; his wife still opposed his idea of a musical career, but Fulson had met people in California who had talked to him about making records, and he was determined to return to the West Coast as soon as he could, with or without Mrs. Fulson.

The Fulsons left for California later in 1946 (they would stay together for three more years), and in that year he made his first record for Bob Geddins, a Texan who had gone west in 1942, he said, "along with thousands of Negroes who left

Texas, Oklahoma, and Louisiana to find work in the wartime shipyards." Fulson labored in the same shipyards until the late 1940s, when he decided no longer to risk injury to his hands and to make music his full-time occupation.

Fulson recorded for many rhythm-and-blues labels in the late 1940s and the 1950s: Big Town, Gilt Edge, Aladdin, and, for eight years, Checker, a subsidiary of Chicago's Chess Records. Jay McShann recorded Fulson for the Swing Time label. Later, Leonard Chess asked him to move to Chicago to record for the Chess label, but Fulson refused because he did not want to live in Chicago and because he did not like the musicians there; accordingly, the record executive arranged for Fulson to hold his sessions (with his own musicians) in a Dallas studio, making the Oklahoma guitarist one of the very few, if not the only, Chess artist to record outside of Illinois.

In the early 1950s, Lowell Fulson led his own West Coast rhythm-and-blues band. Stanley Turrentine, nowadays a noted jazz saxophonist, played tenor for him. And there was a young piano player, a blind singer from Georgia, who was with Fulson from 1950 to 1952—who was with him until Fulson decided he could not pay him what he was worth, until Fulson recognized his potential for individual stardom, until Fulson encouraged him to go out on his own, and until Fulson spoke with record executives about signing the man to a contract with a major label. He was, of course, Ray Charles; he did sign with Atlantic Records; he achieved a level of popularity undreamed of by earlier rhythm-and-blues artists; and he credited Lowell Fulson with starting all of it. Fulson, for his part, continued to record, found fresh audiences for his music in Europe in the 1960s, and would see in the late 1970s and early 1980s the persistence of many of his albums in record-company catalogs.

Oklahomans contributed to the growth of rhythm and blues in ways other than as performers. Take, for example, the Bihari family, siblings Saul, Jules, Joe, Lester, Florette, Roy, and Maxene, children of an Oklahoma farmer who moved the family to California in 1941. The Bihari sons formed Modern Records in Los Angeles in 1945 after Jules Bihari, who worked servicing jukeboxes, discovered how hard it was to obtain rhythm-and-blues recordings. Through Modern and its subsidiary labels like Crown and Kent, the Biharis released the music of Lowell Fulson, Elmore James, John Lee Hooker, Jimmy Witherspoon, Bobby "Blue" Bland, Howlin' Wolf (Chester Burnett), and B. B. King, all certifiable giants of contemporary blues music.

But not all Oklahomans were as successful as the Biharis. Joseph Brown, born in Wagoner in 1904, was a Chicago-based executive, founder of J. O. B. Records in 1949. The company had only one hit record during its existence, and that came in late 1952. Brown could attract none of the major rhythm-and-blues musicians and spent his time merchandising inferior products rather than in developing ties with prominent performers. "The company," Arnold Shaw has noted, "recorded so many little-known artists that Brown branded as a lie the accusation that he would cut [a record for] anybody who paid for a session." Brown died in 1976.

The birth of rock and roll, whether one dates it from July, 1955, when Bill Haley and the Comets reached the top position on *Billboard*'s pop chart with "Rock Around the Clock" or from April, 1956, when Elvis Presley got there with "Heartbreak Hotel," changed the face of American popular music. It happened when white performers discovered rhythm and blues and adapted its sound and even the mannerisms of its musicians to suit their own ends. Elvis Presley, thought in the mid-1950s to be something totally new on the music scene, was merely a white man performing rhythm and blues the way he had watched black artists like Bo Diddly perform it on the stage of New York's Apollo Theater. Whites who had never heard, much less seen, rhythm-and-blues performers would watch Presley on Ed Sullivan's television variety show, and white teenagers, despite the disapprobation of their parents, would embrace the music and the image Presley projected: the sideburns, the pelvic gyrations, the almost arrogant distraction, the apparent moodiness, the implied rebellion against middle-class forms and behaviors. And American popular music was never quite the same again.

The impact of rock and roll on the careers of some Oklahoma musicians was nothing short of devastating. Patti Page, born Clara Ann Fowler in Claremore in 1927, had made her professional singing debut on Tulsa radio-station KTUL in 1946 and was under contract to Mercury Records by 1948. Her recording of "Tennessee Waltz" topped the *Billboard* charts at the end of December, 1950, and remained there through February, 1951. According to *Cash Box* figures, it was the top-selling single in 1951. Her song "I Went to Your Wedding" led *Billboard*'s list from mid-October to mid-November, 1952. And her "Doggie in the Window" was there from mid-March to early May, 1953, ranking as *Cash Box*'s eighth-best-selling single for that year. But rock and roll dislodged Patti Page from those lofty heights. Her "Allegheny Moon" ranked twenty-third in *Cash Box* totals for 1956, behind four different Elvis Presley singles. In 1957 her recording of "Old Cape Cod" was forty-seventh on the *Cash Box* list, again behind four Presley tunes.

Kay Starr was similarly affected. She had made the transition from jazz to pop in the 1950s, with the end of the big-band era, and from mid-March to mid-May, 1952, she had *Billboard*'s number-one song in "Wheel of Fortune" for Capitol Records, the year's sixth-best-selling single. Rock and roll forced yet another transition in her career, but it was only partly successful. She recorded something entitled "Rock and Roll Waltz" for RCA Victor, and it was a number-one recording, but only for the week of February 18, 1956. It was thirteenth on the *Cash Box* list for that year. Neither Page nor Starr would be back,

Patti Page

at least not in the context of an increasingly gimmicky pop music that emphasized novelty for audiences that were fickle with regard to all but the superstars, of which there were surprisingly few. Patti Page had her own television programs on NBC in 1956 and ABC in 1958-59, launched a minor film career in 1960 in Richard Brook's *Elmer Gantry* (earning a larger role in Albert Zugsmith's 1961 *Dondi,* an awful film, and turning in a fair performance in Michael Gordon's 1962 *Boys' Night Out*), and continued to record, for Mercury until 1963, for Columbia until 1970, and back, thereafter, to Mercury. Kay Starr seemed less flexible, moving to guest shots on television in the 1960s but without demonstrating Page's versatility. Her work remained available in record catalogs, however.

Anita Bryant, born in Barnsdall in 1940, and a runner-up in the Miss America contest of 1959, had a brief fling in pop music with 1960's "Paper Roses," number thirty-one on the *Cash Box* list of top-selling singles. But her tours with Bob Hope's Christmas show for American troops overseas (1960-67), her singing of the national anthem for Democratic and Republican conventions (1968), her performances at the White House (1964-69), her membership in the Rev. Billy Graham's evangelistic entourage (after 1965), and her televised plugs for Coca-Cola, Florida orange juice, and Friedrich air conditioners—to say nothing of her concern in the 1970s over sexual preferences of some people in Dade County, Florida—conspired to remove her work from the pop genre. From 1960 on, her songs were, for the most part, either patriotic or religious.

Earl Grant, born in Oklahoma City in 1933, was no chartbuster, and certainly he was no rocker, but as vocalist and pianist he enjoyed a steady popularity among devotees of that variety of music categorized in record stores as "easy listening." Grant recorded two or three albums a year for Decca through the 1960s, until his death in an automobile crash in Arizona in 1970. His 1967 recording of "Ebb Tide" was a million-seller.

Kay Starr

One Oklahoman who achieved momentary fame in the early history of rock and roll was Mark Dinning, born in Grant, south of Hugo near the Red River, in 1933. He was brother to the Dinning Sisters, a vocal group of the 1940s (it was a time for "sisters," e.g. McGuire, Andrews), and so he grew up in a family environment dominated by popular music. He learned to play guitar, and his vocal efforts were enhanced by practice with his sisters; and through the 1950s he worked with several south-western bands. Finally, he recorded a song for MGM Records that stayed at the top of *Billboard*'s pop charts for two weeks in February, 1960. Additionally, it was a hit in Europe and in the British Isles. MGM sold more than a million copies, and the record was sixteenth on the *Cash Box* top-selling list for 1960. The song was "Teen Angel," now accorded the status of "golden oldie" (and, as such, still available on the MGM label) and frequently cited as an archetypal late-1950s, early-1960s young-love-and-sudden-death rock-and-roll lament of the sort popular among self-conscious high-school listeners growing up between John Foster Dulles's nuclear brinksmanship and John Fitzgerald Kennedy's Cuban missile crisis. Dinning could not repeat this success with subsequent releases and so faded from view.

Indeed, given the perverse nature of celebrity, it was a rare performer who did not fade from view in the tumultuous world of rock music. Oklahomans who were band members during the busy years of the 1950s and 1960s must have learned some hard, if not interesting, lessons about management and production in the record business, and about acceptance by critics and the public. Tulsan Bobby Morris was with the Champs (named by Gene Autry after his horse, because the band recorded on an Autry-owned label) when the band had its one big hit, "Tequila," in 1958 — it won a Grammy — and observed the group's subsequent disappearance into record-store golden-oldie bins. Another Tulsan, Steve Hill, was a nineteen-year-old organist with

Bloodrock, a raucous aggregation that began turning its amplifiers up too high in 1969—rock had become more complex in the 1960s, more experimental, less traditional, and louder, too—and went on to earn a deserved reputation as quite possibly the very worst band in the entire history of rock music, its several best-selling albums to the contrary notwithstanding. John Herron, born in Elk City, handled keyboards for The Electric Prunes in the late 1960s and would see their album, *Mass in F Minor,* panned by a critic who said the band sounded like "tone-deaf monks singing Gregorian chants," thus ignoring their obvious achievement in recording a rock album entirely in Latin. And Carl Radle, born in Oklahoma in 1942, performed as bassist with British guitarist Eric Clapton's group, Derek and the Dominos, to produce an album entitled *Layla,* acknowledged not only as one of the top rock collections of 1970-71, but also as one of the best rock albums of all time; and yet, within a year, the much-traveled Clapton had disbanded the group and gone on to other things.

Instability has characterized the history of rock music, insofar as band structure is concerned, more than it has any other form of popular music. From even a cursory examination one gains the impression of almost constant change: new groups supplanting old ones ("old" being often a matter of six months), incessant personnel changes that either decimated bands and prompted their demise or necessitated massive changes of style and repertoire, and so forth. In some instances, change resulted from artistic considerations, but more often it was related to the economics of the rock music industry, which involved record sales and revenue from concert appearances. In no case did anyone seem particularly concerned about the preferences, or even the loyalties, of fans; no, the evidence seemed to indicate that the television generation of the 1970s was predictably fickle, given over to fads that came and went in accordance with the nation's diminished attention span. It was all part of a passing cultural parade, the marchers in which, to paraphrase the complaint of rock-critic Lillian Roxon, would not stand still long enough to have their pictures taken. Specialized publications like *Rolling Stone* appeared to apprise fans of the changes, but there were so many musicians and so much music that the job was difficult at best. Problems were compounded by the growth of recording technology: the number of record labels with national distribution increased dramatically, and locally it was a rare city—or even a fair-sized town—that could not boast of three or four recording studios, though in smaller communities they might be located in the rear of a music store that offered guitar lessons, or out in someone's garage. The technology was available to any who could afford to buy it or rent it. Of the several lessons of the 1970s, one was that anybody could make an album, and anybody usually did.

Analyses of rock music and discographies of rock albums rarely attend to matters of chronology, suggesting the prejudices of rock devotees in favor of a pop culture etched in marble. Whether or not rock music possesses any timeless qualities remains to be seen—it is, after all, a mere three decades old—but meanwhile the parade continues, and the history defies completeness. When someone drops out, then briefly they are remembered and one discovers their whereabouts for all those years. When three members of the rock group Lynyrd Skynyrd were killed in a plane crash in 1977, Oklahomans recalled that two of the victims, Steve Gaines and his sister Cassie, were from Miami—but who knew when they had joined? And when Carl Radle died in 1981, fans were reminded by his obituary that Eric Clapton had fired him as a sideman not long before— had he really been with Clapton for the decade after *Layla?*— and they would remember that Tulsan Jamie Oldaker was now Clapton's drummer—but when had his tenure begun?

And what ever happened to Mike Brewer, born in Oklahoma

City in 1944, the front half of Brewer & Shipley, early 1970s imitators of Simon and Garfunkel whose hit of 1971, "One Toke over the Line," won them a gold record and some imitators of their own? Or how did George Grantham, born in Cordell in 1947, the drummer for Poco, in the late 1960s and early 1970s a band that recalled the ballad tradition in the music of the Southwest, survive all those personnel changes? Or where is John Ware, born in Tulsa in 1944, drummer and keyboard man with Mike Nesmith's First National Band, a minor sensation of the post-Monkees era in the early 1970s? Careful perusal of the small print on the backs of album covers in record stores will provide some answers (John Ware, for example, may be found on several of Emmylou Harris's recent albums; Carl Radle worked for a while with Leon Russell), but the details are obscure in most cases.

Oklahoma has produced some rock artists who have remained in the public eye, including Leon Russell, David Gates, J. J. Cale, and Elvin Bishop. These four were all based in Tulsa early in their musical careers: Russell, Gates, and Bishop were graduates of Tulsa Rogers High School (as was Anita Bryant, coincidentally); and Russell, Gates, and Cale have had careers that intersected more than casually.

Leon Russell was born Russell Bridges in Lawton in 1941 to piano-playing parents who began his lessons in classical music when he was three. The lessons continued for ten years, but Russell stopped them because he wanted to compose his own music and could not do so under the supervision of classical teachers. He was developing also a peculiar piano style, owing to the fact that he had been partially paralyzed at birth and his left hand was stronger than his right; he would cross over on the keyboard, playing melodies with the left hand that other pianists would ordinarily perform right-handed. As a Tulsa Rogers student, he worked in a band formed by Tulsa-native David Gates,

Leon Russell

who was interested in music and in Russell's sister; and during the late 1950s they played at Cain's Ballroom in a trio with drummer Chuck Blackwell, backing visiting rock stars such as Chuck Berry. Russell and Gates were born with perfect pitch and had developed considerable instrumental versatility. Russell had added the trumpet to his musical inventory at age fourteen, and Gates, who had studied piano and violin, knew guitar, organ, and drums. If Gates had any advantage, it lay in his home environment: his mother was a piano teacher and his father was music director for the Tulsa public schools.

At the age of seventeen, having been graduated from high school and deciding against a college education (he told friends he would be too busy making money), Russell traveled to Los Angeles to pursue his musical career. He had to use borrowed identification with an earlier birthdate to find work—a spurious driver's license for a "Leon Russel" gave him his stage name—but because of his talent, to say nothing of his persistence, he was an established studio musician by the early 1960s. As the decade progressed, so did Russell—from one group or solo artist to another, in a succession of studio jobs as staggering in number as they were diverse in musical genre. Russell sided for Paul Revere and the Raiders and Frank Sinatra, the Righteous Brothers and Herb Alpert, the Byrds and Jerry Lee Lewis, Jackie DeShannon and Glen Campbell, and dozens of others.

Gates moved to Los Angeles in 1962, a Tulsa University dropout with a wife and two children and an extensive musical background. He and his family shared a house with Russell, and when the old Tulsa trio (Blackwell was in Los Angeles, too) was not looking for playing dates, Gates did studio work, not only as a sideman but also as an arranger. Within two years Russell and Gates were having serious disagreements about music and about the way Russell lived, the latter conflict developing in part over the constant flow of houseguests that Russell invited to stay in his half of their shared home.

Both men continued their studio work. Russell had plans to launch a studio of his own, and he devoted more and more time to that project after 1967, with some interruptions permitted by close friends. He did a bit of television work and became involved with the musical endeavors of British rock-artist Joe Cocker, working on Cocker's second album and organizing Cocker's American tour of 1970, a chaotic and enormously popular rock melange of forty-two adults and children advertised as "Mad Dogs and Englishmen." The tour was a showcase for Russell's talents, and the feature-length film of 1971 and the soundtrack album it inspired merely extended Russell's reputation. By then, his Shelter label was appearing on his own albums. In 1972 he participated in George Harrison's Grammy-winning *The Concert for Bangla Desh*.

Gates, meanwhile, had improved his lot as well. He went from handling the string arrangements for the Nitty Gritty Dirt Band's recording of 1969 "Buy for Me the Rain" to working with a group named Pleasure Faire. Gates and two members of this band formed a new group, calling themselves Bread, and secured a contract with Elektra Records. Bread's fourth album, *Baby, I'm A-want You,* won a gold record in 1972; and so did Shelter's *Leon Russell & the Shelter People.* And so did Russell's album, *Carney;* and so did Bread's *Guitar Man.* And Bread's *Manna.* And Bread's *On the Waters.* The score for 1972: Bread, five gold records (counting the one for the single release, "Baby, I'm A-want You"); Russell, two. In 1973, Bread won for *The Best of Bread,* and Russell won for *Leon Live.*

Russell returned to Tulsa in 1972 to establish a recording studio for Shelter at Grand Lake. Bread disbanded in 1973 and Gates went on to make solo albums, the critical view being that he was better with the group than he was alone. Bread re-formed in 1977 for a recording date, and periodically thereafter came concert tours announcing "David Gates and Bread," evidently viewed by the participants as the best of both worlds for the satisfaction of fans and egos. Russell left Tulsa again in 1976, returning to Los Angeles to make more records. He continued to be a superb blues performer, even though his voice had always left a great deal to be desired, and he experimented successfully with blending rock and country-and-western music, recording with Willie Nelson and touring with John Hartford and the New Grass Revival. By 1980 he was involved in video production and was considering reopening his Tulsa studio.

Russell's Shelter Records elevated a number of Oklahoma performers to national prominence. One of these was J. J. Cale, a Tulsa guitarist and songwriter who by 1980 had recorded six albums for Shelter and had worked with Russell as a sideman on a number of others. Cale, a year older than Russell, had labored for a decade in Tulsa nightspots as a human jukebox (the metaphor is his), making very little money in the process. He went to Los Angeles and then to Nashville, but without giving much thought to becoming an entertainer. A fine instrumentalist, he proved to be an indifferent singer, and when his records brought him notice and concert bookings, he proved to be an indifferent performer: he was so relaxed that he was boring to audiences who expected to see something happen. He was informal, surely, and fans may have forgotten that he sometimes taped album cuts for Shelter on his back porch in Tulsa. His manner did not adversely affect his popularity, however, and in 1980 he had launched his first major tour of approximately one hundred engagements, including dates in Australasia and Europe.

Elvin Bishop was graduated from Tulsa Rogers in 1960, a rebel with no particular cause. He was a bright—some said brilliant—student, a spelling champion who earned money as a teenager by writing television scripts for low-budget westerns, a nonconformist who excelled at mathematics and physics and English but rarely did his homework, and a disciplinary problem who won a National Merit Scholarship. He collected blues rec-

Elvin Bishop

ords and listened to primitives like John Lee Hooker before it
was fashionable to do so. He spent time in Tulsa's black section, prowling the clubs to hear visiting performers like Duke
Ellington, performers whose presence in town was unknown to
most whites. He played at (as opposed to "played") guitar and
piano, but he knew little about the instruments by the time he
left Tulsa to attend the University of Chicago.

In Chicago, Bishop met Paul Butterfield, who was also interested in blues music. He taught Bishop to play the guitar, and
within two years the Tulsan abandoned the groves of academe
to become a musician. He played rhythm guitar in The Paul
Butterfield Blues Band, remembered by musicologists as the
first electrified white blues group, and he performed on its first
album, released by Elektra in 1965. Bishop left Butterfield in
1968 to start his own band, and by the late 1970s he was
leading a ten-piece group that performed Bishop's good-time
brand of rock and roll and was responsible for more than a
half-dozen albums on the Epic and Capricorn labels. Bishop
was more interested in enjoying himself than in making money,
and stardom was considerably less important to him than lon-
gevity in the fickle world of popular music.

From the perspective of the observer of regional culture, Russell, Gates, Cale, and Bishop have been more faithful to their
musical roots than perhaps even they would care to admit. They
have remained as innovative musicians in a genre that frequently
(but not for long) rewards derivative performances, and it is
undeniable that many have profited in the marketplace by copying their styles. Each has, in his own way, produced contemporary music that harks back to a time when music was the
most important consideration, not the distractions brought on
by an industry madly pursuing the fleeting image of mass appeal.
Russell, Gates, Cale, and Bishop have attracted audiences, but
one cannot say that they have pandered to them, or that they

sought them at the expense of artistic integrity—any more than the jazz musicians of an earlier day did. But the same thing may not be said of other Oklahomans involved in contemporary music.

Many Oklahoma musicians have tried to enter the mainstream of rock music, perhaps without recognizing that popular music is too much of a whore to fashion to offer security to cultural sycophants, and they have failed on the national level because they have been derivative, because they have copied. In the process, they have flailed around (in the cultural sense), looking for the combination that leads to a momentary success which, at the time, seems for all the world to be a permanent thing. The irony is that they are often oblivious to their own seduction by record companies, by the lure of national exposure, and, of course, by the promise of greatly increased revenues. Critics, who have listened to more popular music than any performer (but, one supposes, because they have to, and not because they especially enjoy it), consign them to oblivion, even while the audiences are still listening—surely a confusing situation to the musicians, who imagine that the audiences belong to them and are therefore most definitely not waiting for the next new act.

Dwight Twilley (with fellow-Tulsan Phil Seymour) began his recording career with Shelter in 1975 and produced his best album there, before switching to Arista out of displeasure with Shelter. Tom Petty, also an Oklahoman, and his band, The Heartbreakers, began with Shelter, too. Petty claimed that Shelter was responsible for his lack of success and left the label. When Seymour, having left Twilley and having sided for Petty, decided to strike out on his own, Petty told him to avoid Shelter. Seymour signed with Boardwalk and Petty signed with Backstreet, and both released new albums in 1980-81. Seymour's album was a potpourri of, among other things, New Wave-punk, Beatles, Donovan, and rockabilly sounds. Petty's vocals were rendered

music would be well advised to consult it. There are several good books available on the transition from rhythm and blues to rock and roll (Shaw's *Honkers and Shouters* is one), but an especially useful one is Lawrence N. Redd, *Rock Is Rhythm and Blues: The Impact of Mass Media* (East Lansing: Michigan State University Press, 1974). See also Charles Keil, *Urban Blues* (Chicago: University of Chicago Press, 1966), Charlie Gillett, *The Sound of the City: The Rise of Rock 'n' Roll* (New York: Dell Publishing Co., 1972), and Peter Guralnick, *Feel Like Going Home: Portraits in Blues & Rock 'n' Roll* (New York: Outerbridge & Dienstfrey, 1971).

Earl Bostic (King 5010X) is a "best of" collection of fourteen selections covering Bostic's twenty-year association with the King label. Joe Liggins may be heard on *This Is How It All Began* (Specialty SPS 2117), an anthology, and two Hal Singer tunes, including "Cornbread," are contained on *The Roots of Rock 'n' Roll* (Savoy 2221).

Lowell Fulson's best album is *Lowell Fulson* (Chess 2 ACMB-205), but his later work is represented by *The Ol' Blues Singer* (Granite GS 1006) and *Lovemaker* (Big Town BT-1008). There are no recordings of the Fulson band with Ray Charles, but the pianist's recollections of his years with Fulson may be read in Ray Charles and David Ritz, *Brother Ray: Ray Charles' Own Story* (New York: The Dial Press, 1978).

In addition to the Kay Starr albums listed for the preceding chapter, consult *Patti Page's Greatest Hits* (Columbia CL 2526). Anita Bryant, *Mine Eyes Have Seen The Glory* (Old Tappan, N.J.: Fleming H. Revell Co., 1970), chronicles her move into and out of popular music, and *Anita Bryant's All-Time Favorite Hymns* (Word WST-8652) is representative of what she went on to do.

Earl Grant's work is preserved in *Best of Earl Grant* (MCA 2-4059) and *Best of Earl Grant, Vol. 2* (MCA 2-4096). Mark Dinning, "Teen Angel/ Bye Now Baby" (MGM MVG 522) may still be found packaged as an "oldie" single, but, if not, Dinning is anthologized in any number of collections, including *American Graffiti* (MCA 2-8001), the film soundtrack album; *Oldies But Goodies, Vol. 7* (Original Sound 8857); and *Super Oldies of the Sixties, Vol. 12* (Trip TOP-60-12). The Champs' "Tequila" is contained in *Super Oldies of the Fifties, Vol. 5* (Trip TOP-50-5). The Electric Prunes are represented on *Nuggets* (Sire H-3716). Several Blood-rock albums were available in 1980, with little to distinguish between them. Derek and the Dominos, *Layla* (RSO RS-2-3801), with Carl Radle, is a fine album. Poco, *Pickin' Up the Pieces* (Epic BXN 26460), the group's first and best album, contains some George Grantham vocals. Brewer and Shipley, *Rural Space* (Kama Sutra KSBS2058) is representative.

There is a great deal of Leon Russell material available. *Leon Russell* (Shelter SRL 52007) and *Leon Russell & The Shelter People* (Shelter SRL 52008), the latter with Carl Radle and Chuck Blackwell, are representative of his early work, while *Hank Wilson's Back* (Shelter SRL 52014) and, with Willie Nelson, *One for the Road* (Columbia KC 2 36064) reveal his later interest in country music. David Gates's music is showcased on *The Best of Bread* (Elektra 6E-108); he wrote eight of the album's twelve songs. J. J. Cale, *Okie* (Shelter SRL 52015) is representative; and the title cut was indeed recorded on Cale's back porch in Tulsa. Cale also played lead guitar (with Radle on bass) for Russell's *Hank Wilson's Back*. Elvin Bishop's albums include *Juke Joint Jump* (Capricorn CP 0151); *Struttin' My Stuff* (Capricorn CP 0165); *Home Town Boy Makes Good* (Capricorn CP 0176); and *Hog Heaven* (Capricorn CPN 0215). Although his first work was on *The Paul Butterfield Blues Band* (Elektra EKL-294), the album may prove difficult to obtain.

John Scott, "Their Age of Innocence, Part 1," *Oklahoma Monthly*, May 1977, pp. 23-27, 72-81, discusses Russell, Gates, Bishop, and Anita Bryant in the Tulsa Rogers context. Jan Reid, *The Improbable Rise of Redneck Rock*, discusses Russell (pp. 297-300) and Willis Alan Ramsey's dealings with Russell's Shelter label (pp. 167-82).

Dwight Twilley Band, *Sincerely* (Shelter SRL 52001) features Twilley and Phil Seymour performing vocally and instrumentally on twelve Twilley songs. *Phil Seymour* (Boardwalk FW 36996) and Tom Petty and The Heartbreakers, *Hard Promises* (Backstreet BSR-5160), are the albums to which the text has reference. *20/20* (Epic NJR 36205) and *Gap Band III* (Mercury SRM-1-4003) are instructive on the subject of derivation.

133

10. The Composers

IN 1943, Oklahoma struggled in the throes of an enormous and largely self-inflicted image crisis. It put aside the colorful Indians and cowboys and wildcatters whose myths had stamped, if not the character of the state then certainly its marketable heritage, from the knicknacks of souvenir shops along Route 66 to the postcards sold in every hotel lobby. It forgot Will Rogers for the moment, and Wiley Post, and Jim Thorpe, all of whom had advanced its reputation on the screen or in print. It thrust away virtually every aspect of its substantial culture to embrace—in anger and shame—what it perceived to be the national view of Oklahoma, the vision of the Okie that John Steinbeck presented in *The Grapes of Wrath* in 1939 and John Ford brought to motion-picture theaters in 1940. Oklahoma embraced the image, but not with affection; Oklahoma embraced it, the better to wrestle with it and, if possible, to explain it away. The struggle has continued unabated for more than four decades.

It would be difficult to overestimate the import that Steinbeck's novel of California-bound refugees from depression and dust had, and to some extent continues to have, on Oklahomans. In Oklahoma City legislators spoke out against the book, even those who had not read it. Editorialists castigated the volume in state newspapers. County agents offered impassioned defenses of agricultural conditions in their districts, crying loudly that Steinbeck, an outlander after all, had gotten his facts wrong. The furor was deafening, perhaps because so much of what Steinbeck wrote was true and because so much of what he described had come about because of Oklahomans themselves. Recent studies of the Dust Bowl era indicate that equal parts of avarice and sheer stupidity were responsible for the agricultural calamities of the 1920s and 1930s, no matter how vehement the denials of local politicos and chambers of commerce.

The cultural consequences of the whole era were far-reaching and will be discussed at greater length in the next chapter. At this point, suffice it to say that Steinbeck's book, whether or not it spilled the proverbial beans, was the source of considerable embarrassment and prompted a search by Oklahomans for something to take its place in — no, something to force it from — the national imagination. The Regents of the University of Oklahoma would seize upon big-time football as the panacea for a suffering image: give the people a winning team and they will forget the negativism of alien authors.

The irony is that football promoted the images of the boomer and the sooner, both of whom were, historically, varieties of lawbreakers, flying in the face of authority to avail themselves of federally controlled Indian land in the 1880s and led occasionally by individuals deemed by the U.S. Army to be certifiably unhinged. But that is the trouble with imagery: do away with one image, and you risk acquiring another that is worse. And certainly Steinbeck's Okies were nobler, more principled, and altogether saner than historical characters like David L. Payne. Steinbeck did not portray them as worthless, nor were they, historically. We have seen something of their impact on California, insofar as culture is concerned. Steinbeck always intended to write a sequel, a novel about how the Okies took over California—took it over politically and economically as well as socially. That he did not promptly do so may somehow explain the primacy of football on the Southern Plains.

A degree of salvation came during this crucial period from an unexpected quarter, when, squarely in the middle of the war, two New Yorkers named Richard Rodgers and Oscar Hammerstein II produced a musical entitled *Oklahoma!* for the Broadway stage. Here was a positive statement, a wholesome effort, flattering because it bespoke rural values, exposed a colorful Oklahoma past to seemingly endless audiences, and was based on a play *(Green Grow the Lilacs)* by an Oklahoma playwright (Lynn Riggs). The overwhelming popularity of the musical and its extension of a favorable state image led in 1946 to an official invitation to Rodgers and Hammerstein to visit Oklahoma as honored guests, on the occasion of the first performance by the *Oklahoma!* road company in the state.

Richard Rodgers seemed astonished by the whole thing. True, the musical had garnered all sorts of accolades, including a special Pulitzer Prize in drama in 1944. True, the show offered a new musical format—singing, dancing, and acting all at once. But nothing that eastern audiences and New York critics had said or done could have prepared Rodgers and Hammerstein for what Oklahomans had planned. Governor Robert S. Kerr met their train that November day in 1946 with an entourage that included a surrey with a fringe on top, to transport the guests to their hotel. Unhappily for the hosts, an ice storm forced cancellation of a parade through downtown Oklahoma City, a parade to consist of, Rodgers recalled, "no fewer than forty-seven marching bands and thousands of Indians on horseback." The composer and his lyricist attended the premier Oklahoma performance of their show and a formal ball later. "We were also made honorary Kiowa Indians," Rodgers noted, "and each of us was presented with a chief's headdress."

Eventually, of course, "Oklahoma!" by Richard Rodgers and

Oscar Hammerstein II became the state song. And Rodgers guessed the reason why: "Our show was apparently a great morale booster for citizens of the state who had long been stigmatized by the words 'dust bowl' and 'Okies,' and they did everything they could to show their appreciation."

In his autobiography Richard Rodgers spoke candidly about how he wrote the music for *Oklahoma!* He described the way he deceived audiences into believing that they were hearing authentic Southwestern musical forms—the same procedure he had used to create Siamese music for *The King and I:* from scratch and with no prior knowledge. Hammerstein's fabrications were more extensive and more blatant. He wrote "Oh, What a Beautiful Mornin'" in less than an hour on his Pennsylvania farm, staring at a cornfield from his study window and attempting to estimate its height. At first, he thought it to be as high as a cow pony's eye, but that was not high enough for the image of Oklahoma he wished to portray. Then he tried a giraffe, but that was too high. He split the difference and made it as high as an elephant's eye, later confessing to *Life* magazine that he almost telephoned the Philadelphia Zoo to have an employee go out and measure one for him. Nevertheless, the New Yorker writing in Pennsylvania described corn he had never seen growing in a place he had never seen and helped to immortalize both. The cynic might remark that Steinbeck, at least, had visited Oklahoma and had met the people he was writing about, but never mind: Oklahoma needed *Oklahoma!,* Oklahoma got it in 1943, and Oklahoma has clung to it in one way or another ever since.

This recounting has a point, and it is not to demean the achievement of Rodgers and Hammerstein or to suggest that their musical is somehow flawed. Rather, *Oklahoma!* is but another example of imported culture, a manifestation of that

137

which critics elsewhere have pronounced good and acceptable and therefore worthy of—indeed, it demands—adoration and emulation by Oklahomans. That is a cultural situation that did not exist before the Depression and the hypersensitivity of Oklahomans that developed from it. But it is a situation that has caused Oklahomans to ignore indigenous culture in favor of imports and to overlook the contributions of native sons. If culture in Oklahoma is something that comes from someplace else, then it is only fitting that New Yorkers should write the state song.

But consider for a moment the career of Roy Harris, born on Lincoln's Birthday, 1898, in Lincoln County, Oklahoma Territory. When he died in October, 1979, at the age of eighty-one, he had not been mentioned in Oklahoma history texts, despite having composed sixteen symphonies (one of which was the first by an American composer ever to be recorded) and nearly two hundred other major works. He was a composer who looked to his roots for musical sources, to which his *Folk-Song Symphony* attests. That particular work antedated *Oklahoma!* by three years.

Nor have Oklahomans remembered Gail Kubik, born in South Coffeyville in 1914, a composer who wrote music for armed-forces documentaries during World War II, produced several major film scores, and created the music for "Gerald McBoing Boing," an animated cartoon—one of the best ever made, according to Leonard Maltin—that won an Academy Award in 1951. Kubik received the Pulitzer Prize in music in 1952 for his *Symphony Concertante.* He, too, looked to folk music and also to jazz and other popular forms for inspiration. Properly, Kubik and Harris are classical composers, but because much of their work derived from popular (in the sense that I have earlier defined it) sources, they are also properly included in a discussion of popular music. Inasmuch as their compositions are vibrant and still current reflections of American life and culture, they also recapitulate much of the mood that was present in Oklahoma's early musical environment. Both men's emphasis on the importance of folk songs, for example, reminds us anew of the ballad context of Southwestern musical culture.

One listens to such music and doubts seriously that Oklahoma had to await the efforts of composers from somewhere else.

It was a rare Oklahoma performer who did not write at least some of his own music, and so most of the people mentioned in earlier chapters could rightly be discussed here as well—the jazz artists, the pop singers, the country-and-western musicians, and so forth. But there are several who seem especially suited to this category, either because they are performers who write nearly all of their own material or because they are noted primarily as songwriters, if they perform at all. In most cases, the music they have written has been recorded by a number of other artists, frequently in other musical genres. Therefore, they are a separate and distinct group from people like Patti Page, Jody Miller, Tommy Overstreet, Kay Starr, and Cal Smith, who have built reputations as performers of music that someone else wrote.

Two of the most prolific and influential songwriters Oklahoma has produced are Roger Miller and Hoyt Axton. They have developed distinctive musical styles, both as composers and as performers, and their material has been "covered"—that is to say, recorded subsequent to the original release—by many other musicians. Both have achieved solid reputations and large followings with repertoires of songs that, significantly in view of their regional origins, tell stories.

Roger Miller grew up in poverty in Erick, Oklahoma, raised by an aunt and uncle after his father died and his mother had become desperately ill. His formal education ended after the eighth grade, and as a teenager Miller was both a working cowboy and an occasional rodeo performer, spending his spare time learning to play banjo, piano, and guitar. He enlisted in the army in the early 1950s, and, as a member of Special Services, entertained soldiers stationed in Korea by playing guitar and doubling on fiddle and drums in a country-and-western band. At this point, he began performing songs he had written and was encouraged by their reception.

After his enlistment ended, Miller moved to Nashville, working as a bellhop while he wrote music. He collaborated with singer Bill Anderson in writing "When Two Worlds Collide," which Miller recorded and which became a hit in 1961. When subsequent recordings produced no comparable success, Miller left Nashville to take acting lessons in Hollywood in 1963. He switched also from RCA Victor to the Smash label. By 1964 he had abandoned the acting lessons because he had begun to score on pop charts with new recordings of his own compositions, including "Chug A Lug" and "Dang Me." In 1965 he followed with "King of the Road," perhaps his best-known song, and "Engine, Engine No. 9" and "Kansas City Star."

Twenty-eight-year-old Roger Miller won five Grammy Awards from the National Academy of Recording Arts and Sciences in 1964, all on the strength of "Dang Me." He accomplished even more in 1965 with "King of the Road," garnering six Grammys. Interestingly, Jody Miller, no relation to Roger, but a singer who had grown up in Blanchard and had performed both on Oklahoma City television with Tom Paxton and as a folksinger in several central Oklahoma clubs and coffeehouses, won a Grammy in 1965 for a whimsical "reply" to Miller's hit, entitled "Queen of the House."

Roger Miller also received awards from the Academy of Country and Western Music as 1965's "Man of the Year" and "Best Songwriter." He compiled an enviable list of gold records during the late 1960s and continued to write best-selling tunes.

He did not match that productivity in the 1970s, but his work during the 1960s was sufficient to establish his position in American popular music and to ensure that he would remain in demand for concerts and television appearances. He also helped other songwriters to achieve national prominence when, as an established performer, he recorded their compositions. It was his recording of "Me and Bobby McGhee," for example, that introduced Kris Kristofferson's music to American audiences.

Hoyt Axton, born in Duncan in 1938, became a songwriter through emulation. He has told the story many times of how, as a teenager, he was eating peanut-butter sandwiches in the kitchen while his mother, Mae Boren Axton, nowadays known as the "Queen Mother of Country Music" but then a high-school journalism teacher, sat at the table with a friend collaborating on a song for a young performer she had recently met. Hoyt Axton was present at the creation, as it were, and noted that the whole process required the consumption of four or five sandwiches. The young man Mae Boren Axton had met was Elvis Presley, and the song she cowrote was "Heartbreak Hotel," Presley's first hit recording and, as we saw in the last chapter, a turning point in the evolution of rock and roll.

Hoyt Axton attended Oklahoma State University from 1957 to 1958 and began his career as a professional singer in 1961. Thanks to the successes of performers as diverse as the Kingston Trio, Harry Belafonte, and Joan Baez, the country was in the midst of a folk-music revival (which would build through the decade and intensify along with American involvement in Southeast Asia and under the influence of Woody Guthrie's "children"); and Axton received some attention as a folksinger, portrayed on a now-ancient television semidocumentary as an angry (or at least scowlingly serious) young man driving between coffeehouses in a battered convertible, his guitar tossed casually in the back seat, to sing for patrons his "Greenback Dollar," a song which made its way into many a folk artist's

Hoyt Axton

repertoire during that period, including that of The Kingston Trio.

As time passed, Axton achieved more recognition as a songwriter than as a performer. As late as 1975 he would refer to himself as a "mini-star," a condition of obscurity even then doomed by his own remarkable versatility: he would act in motion pictures (extending a career that reached back at least to 1966 when he played Fess Parker's younger brother in George Sherman's film, *Smoky*) and on television series; he would perform in television variety specials; and he would maintain a busy concert schedule, commensurate with his frequent and popular recordings. But before those things came to pass, Axton's music attracted attention only when rendered by other people.

Rock musicians made especially good use of Axton's tunes and lyrics in the late 1960s. Rock, as a musical genre, was flexing its sociopolitical muscles—it had been doing so since Barry McGuire recorded "Eve of Destruction" in 1965, making it the first rock protest song—and some of Axton's music suited the trend. An amiable, pot-bellied good-old-boy in the 1980s, Axton is seldom assigned a political character and is perhaps not touted as a performer having social concerns, despite the fact that his vita indicates performances of his for charity fundraising events and for prisoners in San Quentin and his political support of presidential hopefuls Eugene McCarthy and George McGovern. In the late 1960s he dealt musically with themes that few had seriously confronted onstage, notably the question of narcotics addiction. Steppenwolf, a rock group with a decidedly political bent, recorded Axton's "The Pusher" in 1968, the first song to treat realistically an obvious social problem. In the early 1970s the group recorded Axton's "Snowblind Friend," a song about the causes and consequences of cocaine use.

"Snowblind Friend" was written in 1968, and so was "Seven Come," an apocalyptic vision of the end of the world and God's sadness over the destructive folly of the human species. But within a few short years, Axton's musical pessimism had abated, and his songs were on the lips of new musicians. Steppenwolf ceased to be in February, 1972, having made its statement, according to its members; but by that time Axton's music was being performed by Three Dog Night (named after the Australian colloquialism for a very cold evening—a night in which a person required the company of only one dog was considerably warmer), a band with poor critical standing but an enormous popular following. Three Dog Night reached the top of the charts in 1971 with Axton's "Joy to the World," a happy bit of musical fluff that introduced a bullfrog named Jeremiah, later to be enshrined as a logo on Axton's own record label. And the band climbed back into the top ten in 1972 with Axton's "Never Been to Spain," wherein he made reference to his Oklahoma antecedents. The popularity of the band and, correspondingly, these two songs provided a substantial boost to Axton's career.

By 1980, Hoyt Axton had nearly twenty albums to his credit and had released a number of singles that had attracted wide notice. His hits included duets with Linda Ronstadt on "When the Morning Comes" and "Lion in the Winter," and with Renee Armand on "Boney Fingers." In 1976 he scored with "Flash of Fire," and in 1979 he had hits with "Rusty Old Halo" and "Della and the Dealer." Nor were Axton's only successes as a recording artist the ones that came with his own songs; his cover of Michael Murphey's "Geronimo's Cadillac" was crisper, cleaner, more intelligible, and more vocally and instrumentally satisfying than Murphey's original.

In the 1970s, Axton traveled in a converted bus he had named "Honeysuckle Rose" and about which he had written a song in 1976. When film producers approached him about a movie, to be named for the bus and revolving around the life and loves of a touring country-music performer, Axton did not approve of the arrangements, and when the film appeared,

144

Willie Nelson starred. The story is instructive because it suggests something about Axton and his music and explains why he has not pursued superstardom with the abandon of some. He has made the point in several ways on several occasions: he will write his songs, and he will sing them, and he hopes you like them. Anything else, as they used to say, would be so much velvet.

Roger Miller and Hoyt Axton have written a number of songs that, in a folk tradition, would be classified as "nonsense songs" —songs featuring Axton's wine-sipping bullfrog and Miller's uncle who "used to love me, but she died," or describing, as one of Miller's did, the impossibility of roller skating in a buffalo herd. Even so, the Oklahoma composer who has produced more nonsense than anyone else must be Sheb Wooley, perhaps best remembered as one of the bad guys in *High Noon* or as Pete Nolan who rode the cattle trails from 1959 to 1965 on CBS television's "Rawhide" series.

Wooley was born in Erick in 1921 and learned country-and-western music during his school years. He was a passable guitarist but a better singer and songwriter, and he performed for a while on Fort Worth radio-station WBAP before forming his own touring band in 1946. He attended acting classes as well as practicing his music, and in the late 1940s he signed a contract with MGM Records and began doing bit parts in films. Both careers accelerated in the 1950s, but here we are concerned with his music.

Early on, Wooley demonstrated a talent for parody that would mark his songwriting career and account for many of his top recordings. Country-music giant Hank Snow recorded Wooley's parody entitled "When Mexican Joe Met Jole Blon" in 1953, and the song, which mingled themes from popular Cajun and Tex-Mex (the name applied to music from the Rio Grande border region) tunes, became a best-seller. Wooley's penchant

145

for nonsense was nowhere more apparent than in his "Purple People Eater," a novelty song about a flying beast with one eye and a single horn that he wrote and recorded for MGM in 1958. It topped *Billboard*'s pop chart for six weeks in June and July of that year and has been frequently resurrected in anthologies of pop music of the 1950s. In 1962, Sheb Wooley had another hit for MGM with "That's My Pa," but in years to come he would be known to audiences by a different name.

In the mid-1960s, Wooley created a vehicle for the presentation of his abundant parodies, an alter ego named Ben Colder (as in, "I been colder, but I don't know when"), a hayseed character remarkable for his disheveled appearance and his none-too-steady manner, both qualities that derived from his inebriated state. Colder was himself a parody, a charming tippler who had trouble standing upright and who slurred and struggled with the words of any song he happend to be singing. He was ideal for Wooley's purposes, inasmuch as Wooley's uncanny talent for parody seemed on the verge of running amok in the 1960s: country music, dealing increasingly with realistic themes and taking itself a bit too seriously in the process, was vulnerable; and, if almost any country song could be parodied, it may be suggested that Wooley (as composer) and Colder (the composer in costume with alcoholic affectation) parodied almost all of them, or certainly almost all of the popular ones. The jibes were light hearted and good natured, and they seemed to emanate more from Colder's disorientation than from any malicious intent on Wooley's part, but, whatever the case, no best-selling country song was sacred.

Wooley, as Colder, poked fun at David Houston's recording of the Billy Sherill-Glenn Sutton song, "Almost Persuaded," voted a Grammy for the best country song of 1966. Houston's performance also earned a Grammy. And Colder's recording of "Almost Persuaded #2" reached the top ten on country charts in the same year. Wooley took on Bobby Russel's Grammy-award-winning "Little Green Apples"—a song of 1968 popularized, incidentally, by Roger Miller—as well as Freddie Hart's country standard, "Easy Lovin," and "Detroit City," a song that won Bobby Bare a Grammy in 1963 and was responsible for starting his career. Even Kris Kristofferson's "Sunday Morning Comin' Down," which had done well for a number of performers, including Johnny Cash, became "Sunday Morning Fallin' Down" in Wooley's boozy translation for Ben Colder. And some songs were ready-made for the Colder image, one of the best being "10 Little Bottles" by Oklahoma singer-composer-actor Johnny Bond.

Interestingly, Wooley managed to get further mileage from "Purple People Eater" by offering a Colder parody of it nearly a decade after the original release—by which time, it might be added in conclusion, Wooley was not only an actor, a composer, and a singer under two names, but also a businessman with two music-publishing houses.

Roger Miller, Hoyt Axton, and Sheb Wooley were originally composers of country or country-inspired material, but their work reached into the pop field, either through their own performances or through those of others who had no country-music background. Their experience was certainly not unique. It was shared, in some unusual ways, by other Oklahoma songwriters.

Merle Kilgore, born in Chickasha in 1934 and raised in Louisiana, was a Grand Ole Opry performer by the time he was eighteen. In 1954 he wrote a song entitled "More and More," predictably a country song and a hit for Webb Pierce, who recorded it; but unpredictably, it also earned a gold record for someone else who recorded it—bandsman Guy Lombardo. Kilgore also wrote "Ring of Fire," a pop hit for Johnny Cash; "Johnny Reb," a top-ten recording for Johnny Horton; and "Wolverton Mountain" for Claude King, a song that has become a country standard and is perhaps the best known of Kilgore's compositions.

Vern Stovall, born in Altus in 1928, was raised in El Reno and Vian, singing in church choirs and at social gatherings and learning to play guitar. He moved to California in 1947 after high school, worked in a Sacramento slaughterhouse and became a butcher, performing after hours on guitar in local nightspots. He met another singer named Bobby George, and they collaborated on several songs. Stovall recorded their composition, "Long Black Limousine," and the tune was subsequently and promptly covered by other performers, including mainline pop-singer Jody Miller, crossover specialist George Hamilton IV, and country-artist Bobby Bare. Elvis Presley released his version in 1969.

Country music is the expected specialty of many Oklahoma composers. To say that there have been prolific country songwriters from the state is to flirt dangerously with understatement, for if we were to examine the output of the most productive country composers, we would find there the credit lines of several native sons, including Floyd Tillman, Wayne P. Walker, Carl Belew, and of course Tommy Collins.

Floyd Tillman was born in Ryan in 1914 and learned to play guitar, banjo, and mandolin from his brothers. In the 1930s he began to perform professionally with various Texas bands, and by mid-decade he was writing and publishing songs of his own. During his long career, he would write hundreds of country tunes, some of which he would record himself, even while other Oklahoma musicians covered them with equal or greater success. For example, Tillman issued his "I Love You So Much It Hurts" for Columbia in 1948 and won a gold record for it; the cover, a duet by singing-cowboys Lloyd ("Cowboy") Copas and Jimmy Wakely occupied the top position on national charts for several weeks during the year. Wakely and Margaret Whiting recorded a best-selling duet of Tillman's "Slippin' Around" and repeated the success in 1949 by releasing Tillman's sequel, "I'll Never Slip Around Again" on the Capitol label. And Tillman did well with his own versions of both the original and the sequel for Columbia. Other Tillman compositions have included "I Gotta Have My Baby Back," "It Makes No Difference Now," and "Each Night at Nine."

Wayne P. Walker was born in Quapaw in 1925, grew up in Texas, served during World War II in the Coast Guard, sold fire escapes in Shreveport, Louisiana, after the war, and became interested in country music through the radio broadcasts of the "Louisiana Hayride." The program was Shreveport-station KWKH's Saturday-night rival of Nashville's WSM Grand Ole Opry broadcasts and was known as "The Cradle of the Stars" because performers who did well on the Shreveport program invariably moved on to Nashville. That was certainly true in Walker's case, although he was a songwriter rather than a performer. But Walker had met Webb Pierce and Red Sovine, two "Hayride" artists who saw promise in his early musical efforts and offered him some needed encouragement. When they went to Nashville, he went too.

Walker's career as a songwriter languished until 1957 when Pierce recorded his "Holiday for Love," Ray Price released his "I've Got a New Heartache," and Carl Smith issued his "Why, Why," all of them hits. Pierce recorded several of Walker's songs, and the Oklahoman's work entered the repertoires of such artists as Patsy Cline, Kitty Wells, and Eddy Arnold. Perhaps because he had been a salesman and knew the importance of volume in any business, Walker believed that productivity was essential to his eventual success as a composer. On the average, he produced a song every three days, and by 1970 he had written more than four hundred, demonstrating a prodigious capacity for work.

One of Walker's early hits of the 1960s was "Hello Out

There," recorded by Carl Belew, himself a songwriter with substantial credentials. Belew was born in Salina in 1931, learned
guitar as a boy, and earned something of a reputation as a
teenage musician in northeastern Oklahoma. He became a
professional musician and paid his dues in a succession of
roadhouses and honky-tonks before his first appearance on
"Louisiana Hayride," which certainly enhanced his regional
standing. Belew was writing some of his own material, but his
big break as a composer did not come through his efforts as
a performer; rather, Belew, like Mae Boren Axton, owed much
to Elvis Presley.

When Presley recorded Belew's "Lonely Street" in the mid-
1950s, the composer's place in the history of popular music
seemed secure. Many other artists covered the song, and Andy
Williams released a hit recording of it in 1959—in fact, the
version released by Williams rather than the Presley one is the
definitive treatment. Belew cowrote "Stop the World," a hit of
1958, and, while Williams was resurrecting "Lonely Street,"
Belew was climbing up the country charts of 1959 with his Decca
recording of another of his songs, "Am I That Easy to Forget?"
Belew moved from Decca to RCA Victor in the early 1960s,
and thereafter he emphasized the performance aspect of his
career. His recording in 1962 of Walker's "Hello Out There"
crossed over to pop charts and was the title of a Belew album
of 1964. Carl Belew released dozens of singles and four or
five albums in the 1960s, but as a performer he evidently was
that easy to forget. As a composer, however, he had produced
memorable popular music.[1]

Tommy Collins, possibly the most prolific of all the Oklahoma

[1]James Talley, born in Mehan in 1944, who recorded four albums for
Capitol between 1975 and 1977 and performed at Jimmy Carter's Inaugural
Ball, had faded into obscurity by 1979, and all of his albums were out-of-print
by 1981. Such are the vagaries of the music business. Belew's experience was
not atypical.

country-music composers, was born in Oklahoma City in 1930. He sang and played guitar in high school and at Central State College (now University) and subsequently on several Oklahoma City radio and television stations. A contract with Capitol Records encouraged him to move, as so many Oklahomans had before (though for different reasons) to Bakersfield, California; and there he made the acquaintance of several notables, Merle Haggard among them. Indeed, in 1981, Haggard acknowledged his debt to Collins and chronicled their friendship in a song entitled "Leonard"; and while "Leonard's" identity may have puzzled some, it was no secret among Oklahoma disc jockeys.

The mid-1950s were successful years for Collins. His first hit recording, "If You Ain't Lovin', You Ain't Livin'," came in 1953. He won awards from *Cashbox* and *Billboard* in 1954, and his recording of his own "You Better Not Do That" sold better than a half million copies. Polls designated him country music's most promising male vocalist in 1955. And so forth. His records sold well, and the compositions continued to flow from his pen. By 1970, Collins had written more than eight hundred songs.

It should be clear by now that contemporary American music owes much to the efforts of Oklahomans—to those composers mentioned here and those discussed in previous chapters, the Jimmy Rushings, the Tom Paxtons, the Leon Russells, and the rest. And yet to this already long list of names there are still others to add, others without whom no survey of popular music would be complete.

Lee Hazlewood, born in Mannford in 1929, collaborated with a guitarist named Duane Eddy to produce "Rebel Rouser," a hit of 1958 that ushered in the era of the "twangy guitar" in American pop. In the late 1960s he joined Nancy Sinatra (whose vocal credentials came not only from her famous father but also from five years of voice lessons with classicist and prize-winning composer Gian Carlo Menotti, whose work Hazlewood labored

151

to undo, thinking Sinatra's voice too high and pure for pop music) in a series of duets that proved extremely appealing to country and pop audiences alike. These included "Summer Wine" and "Jackson" and marked renewed interest in boy-girl vocal repartee in fact, "Jackson" was quickly covered by June Carter and Johnny Cash, who would soon marry: for fans, the barbed exchanges in the duet may have added spice to the publicized romance. Hazlewood and Sinatra released albums in 1970 and 1972, the first one earning a gold record. As a record producer, a music publisher, and a songwriter, Hazlewood occasionally formed groups or cultivated new artists, wrote material for them, and supervised their recording sessions.

Mike Settle, born in Tulsa in 1941, had a varied career that began in folk music and moved into the pop field. He had performed in Oklahoma coffeehouses during the folk revival of the late 1950s and early 1960s, and had left the state for a date at New York's Bitter End, a popular club for folk enthusiasts. A singer and guitarist, Settle was also a songwriter, and he provided material for some prominent folk groups of the period. One may not, of course, "compose" folk music, but the label popularly applied to the polished (which is to say, nonethnic) music performed by Peter, Paul, and Mary, by the Limeliters, and by The Brothers Four was "folk," and those groups used Settle's songs.

Settle joined the Cumberland Three, one of many folk groups spawned by the success of the Kingston Trio, in the early 1960s; and a few years later he became a member of the New Christy Minstrels, a larger and slicker group of musicians who sold millions of albums during the revival years. Much traveled and well versed in the genre, Settle became musical director of the Minstrels, but he was not to remain long with the group.

Settle left the Minstrels in 1967 with Thelma Camacho, Terry Williams, and Kenny Rogers to form a new group and perform, not folk music but a blend of folk, country, and rock that was classified as rock but was more mellow, less abrupt, and more likely to generate crossover tunes for the pop market. Together, they became Kenny Rogers and The First Edition and were trend-setters in the late 1960s, producing hit after hit on record charts and gaining a syndicated weekly television program. Settle continued to write songs, but not the folk-oriented pieces like "Sing Hallelujah" that had marked his early career; now he was attuned to the pop-rock market. Settle left The First Edition in the 1970s to write for television; and, while he would from time to time produce new songs for the group, he would be remembered as the composer of one of its early hits, and indeed one of its best recordings, "But You Know I Love You," a song covered by other performers and as recently as 1981 reissued by country-pop artist Dolly Parton.

Perhaps Jimmy Webb's career has been the most meteoric of any Oklahoma composer's. His phenomenal popularity as a songwriter was based on a rapid succession of blockbuster hits by established performers in the late 1960s; but, when Webb decided to sing his own material, he disappeared from the musical scene in the mid-1970s almost as quickly as he had arrived. A part of the explanation may lie in Webb's belief that he had accomplished all the goals he had established for himself by the time he was twenty-one years of age; he had to do something thereafter, of course, and he hoped to continue to grow musically, creatively. He believed that too many composers settled into a pattern in their writing, the pattern dictated by their successful songs. Webb consciously broke away from the forms and formats that his success imposed, struck out in new directions, and lost—seemingly—both his momentum and his audience. Some critics decried his talents as a performer, but it was impossible, certainly, to ignore what he had achieved as a composer. For Webb's part, he declared in a song of 1976 entitled "If You See Me Getting Smaller I'm Leaving" that it was his right to disappear from the public eye.

Webb was born in Elk City in 1946, the son of a Baptist minister. He was a schoolboy student of piano and organ, assisting his father in worship services, and eventually becoming the choir accompanist. By the time he was thirteen, he was composing his own music. Seven years later, he enrolled in college in California to earn a degree in music; he left before the end of his first year, tried to find work in Hollywood, and eventually hired on at miserable wages at a Los Angeles recording studio.

Singer Johnny Rivers befriended Webb and included Webb's "By the Time I Get To Phoenix" on an album he released early in 1967. Rivers also introduced Webb to the Fifth Dimension, and they used his song "Up, Up and Away" in an album they released in midyear. By that time, Glen Campbell had listened to Rivers's version of "By the Time I Get to Phoenix" and released his cover of it at the end of 1967.

Webb won Grammy Awards for both songs in 1967 and 1968, Trans-World Airlines secured rights to "Up, Up and Away" as a theme song for its advertising, and the machinery that would make Jimmy Webb a millionaire was in motion. In 1968 the group Brooklyn Bridge scored with Webb's "The Worst That Could Happen" and British actor Richard Harris recorded Webb's "McArthur Park," a hit for Harris and later for country music's Waylon Jennings. In 1969, Webb provided Glen Campbell with "Wichita Lineman" and "Galveston," both million-selling hits. Webb was by then involved with several projects, including writing film scores; he was wealthy, but it cannot be said that he was particularly happy about it. Next came his attempts to perform his own music, and eclipse followed.

Composers, no less than performers, are subject to the whims of the music-buying public and, accordingly, to the faddishness of the music industry. But a song, even more than a performance, is also subject to preservation and, accordingly, to resurrection by artists of succeeding generations, frequently or infrequently, as the case may be. As works of creative imagination, they are not lost; and if, as we suggested with Woody Guthrie's songs, they are not timeless then they are at least documents of the time in which they are created.

Oklahoma songs like "Swing Low, Sweet Chariot" by Uncle Wallis Willis and Aunt Minerva perhaps represent the timeless. Others, like Woody Guthrie's "Talkin' Dust Bowl Blues," certainly are documents. Still others may fall somewhere in between and are numbered as genre "standards," basic to the repertoire of a time and place but applicable in other contexts as expressions of some facet of the human condition.

Woody Guthrie chronicled an important aspect of the American experience during the 1930s, as did Sis Cunningham and other rural Oklahoma performers. The work of Gene Autry, Bob Wills, and others bespoke still more about the 1930s. But an even better picture of the decade may be gained by adding to their songs the compositions of people like Albert E. Brumley and Pinky Tomlin. Brumley, born in Missouri, grew up, according to Tulsa historian Guy Logsdon, on his father's farm near McAlester; and in the late 1920s, chopping cotton and noting the walls of the state penitentiary, he formulated the beginnings of a gospel song. He admitted to being influenced by Guy Massey's "The Prisoner's Song," published in 1924 and popular among rural audiences because of Vernon Dalhart's recording of it, but Brumley's song percolated for several years before he published it in 1932. Entitled "I'll Fly Away," it not only remains a country-gospel standard, but it is also taken to be a much older song. Brumley would go on to connect the fact of rural electrification, the growth of radio, and the popularity of gospel programs among rural audiences in "Turn Your Radio On," published in 1938.

Pinky Tomlin, born in Arkansas but raised in Durant, was a banjo-playing farmboy who performed briefly with Louis Armstrong in the 1920s, worked his way through the University of Oklahoma, went to Hollywood and appeared in more than a dozen films in the 1930s, and eventually became involved in the oil business. Between college and the oilfield, however, were a number of years in which Tomlin was in demand as a performer; and that was because of his songs, songs that captured another aspect of the 1930s. Tomlin's compositions included "The Object of My Affection," "What's the Reason I'm Not Pleasin' You?" and "The Love Bug Will Bite You If You Don't Watch Out." So popular were they that they were likely to appear almost anywhere, and sometimes in unexpected places. For example, Darla Hood (born, coincidentally, in Leedey) sang "The Love Bug Will Bite You If You Don't Watch Out" in a Hal Roach *Our Gang* comedy short, wedding Tomlin's work to the cinematic response to Depression-era America in one of those unforgettable kiddie production numbers, cute and telling and altogether fantastic.

And yet, from this array of talent there comes no writer with the lyrical punch of an Oscar Hammerstein II, no composer with the sure hand of a Richard Rodgers? Perhaps not, if culture is that which comes from elsewhere, or if the Broadway stage is the sacred measure of merit. But if I may be allowed an opinion (in a book that bears the label of history but is necessarily polemical since it points to oversights), I would suggest that Oklahomans are more than capable of producing their own music, and that they have written songs more descriptive of the history, culture, and mood of their state than any composed by New Yorkers, South Carolinians, or anybody else imported for the job. I would have thought that something like "Oklahoma Hills," written by Woody Guthrie in the 1930s and popularized by his cousin, country-singer Jack Guthrie, in the 1940s, would have been appropriately jaunty, complimentary, and nostalgic — and certainly more in keeping with Oklahoma's musical heritage than anything to be found in the entire *Oklahoma!* score. And of course I say that, knowing that it will be lost on the sensitive few who selected as the slogan for Oklahoma's Diamond Jubilee the Rodgers and Hammerstein line, "You're doin' fine, Oklahoma." But then, culture ignored is culture lost, is it not?

Sources

Martin Staples Shockley, "The Reception of *The Grapes of Wrath* in Oklahoma," *American Literature* 15:4 (January 1944):351-61, describes state reaction to Steinbeck's book, while Timothy P. Donovan, "Oh, What a Beautiful Mornin': The Musical, *Oklahoma!* and the Popular Mind in 1943," *Journal of Popular Culture* 8:3 (Winter 1974):477-88, and Richard Rodgers, *Musical Stages: An Autobiography* (New York: Random House, 1975), chap. 16, discuss aspects of the New York salvation of Oklahoma's image. *Oklahoma! The Original Broadway Cast Album* (MCA-2030) is the relevant recording. See also the sources for chapter 11.

The works of Roy Harris are widely available. Representative recordings include *Symphony No. 3* (RCA ARL 1-1682); *Folk-Song Symphony* (Angel S-36091); and *Harris Conducts Harris* (Varese Sarabande VC 81085). Gail Kubik, *Symphony Concertante* (CRI SD 267), is a basic item.

Roger Miller's *Dang Me* (Smash SL-7002) and *Best of Roger Miller* (Mercury 61631) contain his best-known compositions. Hoyt Axton's discography is enormous and includes *My Griffin Is Gone* (Columbia KC 33103); *Less Than the Song* (A&M SP 4376); *Snowblind Friend* (MCA 2263); *Life Machine* (A&M SP 3604); *Southbound* (A&M SP 4510); *Fearless* (A&M SP 4571); and, on his own label, *"Where Did the Money Go?"* (Jeremiah JH 5001) and *Rusty Old Halo* (Jeremiah JH 5000). Sheb Wooley's parodies may be sampled on *Ben Colder "Golden Hits"* (Gusto GT-0051).

Several compositions by Oklahoma songwriters may be found in Dorothy Horstman, *Sing Your Heart Out, Country Boy* (New York: E. P. Dutton & Co., 1975), an interesting book with a large discography listing alternate versions of songs. Horstman included brief statements, gleaned from interviews and correspondence with the composers or their families, about how the songs were written. The volume supplements the biographical directories of country performers listed for earlier chapters. Recordings featuring songwriters as performers include *Merle Kilgore* (Mercury 13661); *Floyd Tillman's Best* (Columbia HL-7316); *Twelve Shades of Carl Belew* (RCA LPM-3919); and *This Is Tommy Collins* (Capitol T-1196), all of which may be difficult to find. The version of Stovall's "Long Black Limousine" with the additional Oklahoma connection is on *The Nashville Sound of Jody Miller* (Capitol ST-2996). Here, as elsewhere, anthologies may be useful. *Country Hits of the '40s* (Capitol SM-884) contains the Whiting-Wakely version of Floyd Tillman's "Slipping Around," with, as a bonus, Jack Guthrie performing his and Woody's "Oklahoma Hills," and *Country Hits of the '50s* (Capitol SM-885) includes Tommy Collins singing his "You Better Not Do That" and Faron Young's version of Collins's "If You Ain't Lovin' You Ain't Livin'."

On James Talley, see Guralnick, *Lost Highway,* pp. 248-63. His albums, consisting entirely of Talley compositions evoking, in part, his Oklahoma childhood and the Southwestern landscape, are *Got No Bread, No Milk, No Money, But We Sure Got a Lot of Love* (Capitol ST-11416); *Tryin' Like the Devil* (Capitol ST-11494); *Blackjack Choir* (Capitol ST-11605); and *Ain't It Somethin'* (Capitol ST-11695).

Information on Lee Hazlewood and his association with Nancy Sinatra comes from *Lillian Roxon's Rock Encyclopedia,* which contains partial discographies of his recordings and his recordings with her, but all of the albums are difficult to obtain. Mike Settle's "But You Know I Love You" is on Kenny Rogers and The First Edition, *Greatest Hits* (Reprise 6437). Jimmy Webb's pop classics are likely to be found almost anywhere; his own recordings of his music include *Land's End* (Asylum 5070), *El Mirage* (Atlantic SO 18218), and *Angel Heart* (Columbia FC 37695). Albert E. Brumley's songs have been widely recorded and are discussed in the Horstman book. Jesse Burt and Duane Allen, *The History of Gospel Music* (Nashville: K & S Press, 1971), contains a biographical section which includes Brumley and other Oklahoma gospel composers like Doy Willis Ott and Gary McSpadden; the book concerns white gospel music and places it in a country-music context. For Pinky Tomlin's career, see his *The Object of My Affection: An Autobiography* (Norman: University of Oklahoma Press, 1981).

158

11. The Weight of the Past

THE Depression of the 1930s is rarely mentioned in histories of Oklahoma; and, if it is, the historian frequently hastens on to other things which, if they are not any more pleasant, are certainly less controversial. For to speak of the Depression is to recall Steinbeck, *The Grapes of Wrath,* dust, emigrants—in short, the entire range of unpleasant images that many Oklahomans would prefer to ignore, if not to forget. There is seemingly little interest in analyzing the period or evaluating its consequences. In the words of the author of a popular Oklahoma-history text, the Depression "was just a phase we went through." It could thus be dismissed as a topic for study. World War II, which did not last nearly as long, could be omitted from the history curriculum on the same grounds, of course, and so the statement is absurd. Yet it points to the fact that Oklahomans have contrived a defective history, and one that cannot possibly explain the cultural change that has occurred in their state.

One need not dwell on the hardships of the 1930s to note their impact on Oklahoma culture, an impact that we have measured to some extent in these pages—the reaction to the Dust Bowl image and the compensatory behavior it fostered. In later years, Oklahomans did not demonstrate the xenophobia often anticipated in rural areas; indeed, friendliness and acceptance mark the Oklahoma character to such an extent that newcomers to the state are often moved to comment on the fact. The fear has not been of outsiders but rather of the opinions and judgments of outsiders, and it has had dire consequences for Oklahoma's culture.

When one fears the opinions of an outsider, one may attempt to discover what that outsider views favorably and then try to provide it as a means of gaining approval. Thus the Regents may indeed have spoken to George Lynn Cross about the importance of a winning football team as a way of making Oklahomans feel better about themselves; but the "winning" would have been unimportant if it had not been viewed and applauded by the nation that had read Steinbeck. And of course the sport selected was one in which competition was deemed important on a national level, which is why no one at the meeting suggested a winning lacrosse team, a winning water-polo team, or a winning field-hockey team. Thus, an Oklahoma governor may indeed have arrived at a train station in an antiquated vehicle to meet the successful writers of a successful musical that offered a favorable, if wholly fantastic, image of the state; but it is doubtful that he would have done so for the creators of a Broadway flop, or that the public schools would have closed for the occasion, or that any tune by critical failures would have become the state song. And thus the student or the casual reader who reaches for an Oklahoma-history text may indeed find a chapter on culture; but it will be the last and shortest of all the chapters, it will speak highly of the symphony and the ballet, and it will ignore Woody Guthrie and nearly everyone else mentioned in this book.

The Depression of the 1930s marked the real division between the nineteenth and twentieth centuries in Oklahoma history, if we eschew chronology in favor of attitude. There was in the nineteenth century an unquenchable optimism, growing from the westward movement and the world-beating sense of mission that people had when they set out to subdue a continent. That optimism engendered cultural vitality and economic vigor during Oklahoma's territorial period—why move to the West, why participate in a land run, why abandon a known past for an unknown future unless you truly believe that better things will result?—and it prevailed through the 1920s and early 1930s. Economically, it led to a certain recklessness that resulted in abuse of the land for the sake of profit, as Donald Worster has recently shown, and so it contributed much to the disaster of the 1930s. Thereafter, caution prevailed. Culturally, it led to innovation and fed an environment bubbling already with the creativity that derives from a mingling of diverse customs, and so it contributed to many things: the development of jazz, the unabashed radicalism of the folk tradition, the whole socialization process inherent in community involvement in musical culture. But somehow, by the 1940s that environment had changed.

The cultural consequences of the Depression were more serious than the economic ones, from the perspective of the 1980s. Economically, there was recovery in the 1940s. Culturally, there was not. The cultural environment that had existed in Oklahoma since the 1890s was demolished in the 1930s by economic forces attendant upon or resulting from the Depression, and by the time recovery could have occurred, there seemed no longer to be any need for it among its previous consumers.

The Depression brought an end to the jazz bands of the 1920s, the bands that had survived in Tulsa and Oklahoma City on the revenues of dances in those cities or in smaller outlying communities. The audiences were still there, but they could no longer pay. The Oklahoma City Blue Devils went, one by one, to Kansas City to the cultural haven that was ironically the by-product of corruption and vice. Bob Wills and the Texas Playboys, connected to audiences not only by personal appearances but through radio broadcasts and recordings, fared better; yet the attraction of a California grown prosperous in wartime proved too great to allow Wills to remain in Oklahoma. The audiences of Southwesterners to be found in California, audiences of blacks as well as whites, people now employed and with money in their pockets, contributed something to the lure of the place for performers like Wills and Lowell Fulson. The failed clubs and dance halls of Oklahoma, their doors closed in testimony to hard times, were no inducement to remain.

Many things changed between the 1930s and the 1950s, of course, and not just in Oklahoma. As we have seen, radio stations came to depend less upon live-music broadcasts and more upon recordings. Audiences found new attractions nationally, as evidenced by Basie's reorganization and reduction of his orchestra in the early 1950s. The musical "action" in America seemed to be polarized between New York and California—and Nashville, for country performers; but even its primacy was eroding—and it was to these places that Oklahoma musicians gravitated. The musical crossroads that had served to stimulate Oklahoma's cultural environment by continually introducing fresh elements now became an avenue of departure for local talent in search of opportunity. Because the music industry increasingly promised national exposure, utilizing radio, television appearances, and concert tours to promote record sales (and thus fame and money comprised the bottom line of the promise), such outlets as could be found in Oklahoma for musical expression served most often as training grounds—and provided valuable experience—for performers who hoped to go elsewhere. To some extent, that had always been true: recall Gene Autry's initial abortive trip to New York and his return to Oklahoma to gain experience, events that antedated the worst years of the Depression. But in the late 1940s and the 1950s and beyond, the process intensified—the coffeehouses of the late 1950s and early 1960s, for example, that showcased the talents of Tom

Paxton, Jody Miller, and Mike Settle, were only preparing them for something else.

After the Depression it was nearly impossible for a performer to make a living in Oklahoma from music alone. There were, for one thing, fewer opportunities to work. For another thing, the competition for available places was keener than it had been before, perhaps because there were more and better musicians around than there had ever been before. There was, after all, a national standard of performance, vocally and on any given instrument, and it was on perpetual display through television and radio. Young musicians became adroit at copying both the substance and the style of the national model (as electronic media led the nation along the road to homogenized culture), and they became extremely talented in the process, not because of what they copied but because of how they did it. The teenager listening to a record perhaps did not realize that Chet Atkins or some other musical phenomenon had achieved the desired sound through overdubbing—laying down a track of bass rhythm and then playing the melody on a separate track on top of it—and in any case he did not have the electronic equipment to assist him; so he copied the sound with only eight fingers, two thumbs, and a cheap Sears guitar, improvising to duplicate what it had required thousands of dollars in technology to create in the first place. The trouble was that tens of thousands of other teenagers were doing exactly the same thing. With little to distinguish between one talented musician and another, the whims and fads of the monied entertainment industry made the crucial decision, and intangibles like "breaks" and public acceptance weighed more heavily upon the creation and extension of culture than they had before.

But how long must one wait for the big break? How long must talent languish in the absence of opportunity for expression? And how many received the big break only to face, in turn, the national rejection of their effort? Since World War II for every Oklahoma performer who left the state and found success elsewhere there are dozens who either never had the chance to leave or who were forced by the economic realities of cultural dissemination in postwar America to return and find something else to do.

There are places to perform in Oklahoma, and there are studios in which to make recordings. But the places nowadays are highly specialized and stratified and cater to smaller audiences than those available before the Depression. There are superb bands in Oklahoma—generally rock groups or country-and-western bands—that perform before weekend crowds of around two hundred persons and whose members may have traveled halfway across the state to earn as little as twenty-five dollars for four or five hours of work. Many of these groups have recorded albums, primarily for local consumption, and most have faithful (but small) followings of regular patrons at this or that bar or club. But the work is not steady, because there are not enough clubs or regular patrons, and the musicians must find other jobs. Some operate music stores, some give music lessons, some manage to find part-time jobs of one kind or another, waiting for the weekend and the work they do best. They are professional musicians and thus they describe themselves. Some earn money as session players in studios in Tulsa and Oklahoma City, an occupation of which they, as professionals, are not particularly enamored because the people whom they back are often rank amateurs. "Do you know how to find a recording studio in Oklahoma City?" asked one session player. "You stand on the corner and watch for a big white bus that says 'The So-and-so Family Gospel Singers and Revival Show.' Then you follow it."

For these professionals, who perform for a few dollars a night, Oklahoma recapitulates culturally the era of the Depression each and every day.

164

Terry Ware was born in Shattuck in 1950, grew up in Woodward, learned to play guitar, and became a professional musician in 1965. He attended the University of Oklahoma and took his degree in journalism, studying writing with Foster-Harris and Jack Bickham. After graduation, he moved to Red River, New Mexico, and met, among other musicians, Hugo-born Ray Wylie Hubbard, a singer-guitarist then living in Texas. He and Hubbard performed as a duo in 1972, and, in 1973, Hubbard formed a band that would become known as The Cowboy Twinkies, a rock-influenced group more often associated with the music of Austin, especially after Hubbard's authorship of "Redneck Mother" and Jerry Jeff Walker's popularization of it. Ware was the original Twinkie, and he was joined by some other Oklahoma musicians: Jim Herbst, born in Oklahoma City in 1950, played drums and doubled on keyboards and guitar for Hubbard. The bassist was Dennis Meehan, born in New Hampshire and raised in Oklahoma.

Ware, Herbst, and Meehan stayed with Hubbard until the late 1970s. The band was on the road much of the time, touring with and fronting for performers like Willie Nelson, making two albums with Hubbard, and learning a great deal about the music business. Its members also made a great deal of money, much of which they invested in recording equipment. When the group left Hubbard — some were simply tired of the travel, while others attributed the break to Hubbard's manager and Hubbard's own desire for a larger share of the band's revenue — Ware, Herbst, and Meehan settled in Norman. Ware and Herbst would establish a local band, The Sensational Shoes, which would include bassist Marlin Butcher, born in Oklahoma City in 1951, and drummer Bill Shelton, and occasionally Steve Weichert, a Tulsa-born singer-songwriter-guitarist. Meehan and Herbst would open a recording studio in Herbst's home, and they would both produce and perform on their albums and those made by other local groups, including Oklahoma City-based bands like Xebec and The Lienke Brothers City Band. Meehan and Herbst would engineer the recordings, while Ware and the others were available for session work.

Naturally, there was no money in it, and certainly there were no paydays to compare with what they had known on tour with Willie Nelson. Professionals who had made several thousand dollars a week as nationally headlined musicians were, by 1979, earning perhaps seventy-five or a hundred dollars a week performing locally, not because—and this deserves emphasis, owing to what has gone before—they had not succeeded outside of Oklahoma. Indeed, they had. They returned to Oklahoma because they wished to live there, to pursue their careers there—and yet, they would find this extremely difficult to do. Marlin Butcher, another veteran of the road, supported himself by operating a music store in Lindsay and giving guitar lessons. Herbst, too, worked in a Norman music store. Meehan occasionally clerked in a record shop.

Curiously, the experience of these musicians recalled the Depression era in more ways than one. The Sensational Shoes was, like the Oklahoma City Blue Devils of a half-century before, a commonwealth band, in which hirings and firings and bookings were decided by majority vote and all proceeds were divided evenly among the members. The name of the group derived from the intention of its musicians to play whatever particular audiences wished to hear; for country-music audiences "we put on our boots. For other people, we might wear our rock-and-roll shoes," Herbst explained. The band played blues, country and western, country rock, hard rock, and permutations and variations thereon; and it performed a great deal of original material. Weichert wrote prolifically, and Ware and Butcher collaborated on tunes.

Enjoyment of music seemed of paramount importance to the

Shoes, but the economics of the band's situation cast a shadow over all of that. Shelton, with a family to support, left in 1980 for a better-paying job with a club combo in Oklahoma City. Herbst then took over the drums, and Kenny Phillips joined the band to handle the keyboards. Early in 1981 the group abandoned Weichert, an intense, remote, and humorless performer with an excellent singing voice, because, they said, his personality was putting a damper on things — leading to the perhaps justifiable conclusion that when you work for peanuts you had best have fun doing it. Meehan wanted to go to New York to find a job as a studio engineer, which necessitated the dissolution of the Norman studio after three years of operation; and besides, Herbst was tired of having traffic in and out of his home at all hours. Then Herbst left the Shoes to join Mountain Smoke, originally a bluegrass band that turned to country music and was good enough to be exclusive; Herbst would work weekends with Mountain Smoke, which played primarily for private parties, and make considerably more money than he could with the Norman group. "It's a strange thing about this band," Ware observed of Herbst's departure, "but whenever things start going well, when we're playing well, somebody leaves." Undaunted, The Sensational Shoes set about finding a new drummer and preparing for summer playing dates in Ada and Ware's hometown, Woodward.

And what does Terry Ware wish to be doing ten years hence? "I hope it has something to do with music," he told me in March, 1981. "I'm sort of waiting for something to happen." That is not as aimless as it sounds; Ware was waiting for something to happen when he met Ray Wylie Hubbard, and all those years on the road are now behind him. He has traveled across the country, and he gained a good idea of what he wanted in the process. "I want to live in Norman. I want to do more studio work; I enjoy that. I would like to do more recording." Ware had by then completed work on his first album, entitled *Caffeine*

Dreams, which appeared in the early summer of 1981. It was a virtuoso performance, supported by Herbst, Shelton, Butcher, and Meehan; and it revealed Ware's versatility, demonstrated on several original compositions, a Frank Zappa experimental piece, and a Bach invention. He was elated when a local radio station added the album to its playlist, so minimal are the expectations of contemporary Oklahoma musicians. Speaking of precisely that situation, Herbst remarked that the people of Oklahoma were "lucky to have the talent they've got here. If they keep ignoring it, they won't have it much longer."

Herbst is correct, of course. The quantity of local talent available on any Saturday night is truly impressive, but its existence is almost totally unknown among the inhabitants of the communities in which these musicians perform. In the small bars and clubs where they work, live music is almost an afterthought; there are no bandstands, no stages, not even a riser; the quarters are cramped, and the acoustics are generally awful. So fragile is the hold these musicians have on economic survival, that the disco craze of a few years ago was a direct threat to their security. A club could hire a disc jockey to play recordings over a sound system for less than it cost to employ a band, in the same way that radio stations found it cheaper to air recorded music forty years ago; and disco stood to reduce still further the number of places that state musicians could perform. And yet, as professionals, the musicians struggled on.

Versatility is a hallmark of contemporary Oklahoma bands. It is a strategy devised for survival in a depressed area wherein one may not afford the luxury of overspecialization.

Bob Moore, Keith Mellington, Blair Montgomery, and Terry Gill formed a band called Moon Dog in 1976 in Oklahoma City. Saxophonist Montgomery and banjo-player Gill were Oklahoma City natives, while drummer Mellington came from Okemah; bassist-guitarist Moore was from Abilene, Texas. Another commonwealth band, Moon Dog also shared living quarters, making homes for wives and children in the same three-story house in Oklahoma City.

Moon Dog found work enough to fill fifty weeks of each year, but not in Oklahoma City or even in Oklahoma. The band selected Oklahoma City as its headquarters because "it's centrally located," according to Gill; but most playing dates were in Kansas, Arkansas, and Texas. In the late spring of 1981 the band headed north for a fifteen-week tour of Canada, its fifth Canadian tour in five years. Such peregrinations are indeed reminiscent of the old Blue Devils. There was one club, The Rose, in Oklahoma City where the band performed on a regular basis, but only one night in midweek and then generally for close friends and loyal fans. There was not much money to be made in Oklahoma City, Gill told me, but Tulsa was a better "scene," and the band performed there often.

Country-and-western musicians contended in the early 1980s that Oklahoma City was the place to be for their kind of music, not Tulsa; there were too few places in Tulsa to hear the country sound. Moon Dog, however, survived the effects of that sort of market categorization with its own brand of versatility. How would one, to judge by first appearances, classify a four-piece band in which the pieces are bass, drums, banjo, and saxophone? The delightful thing about culture is its unpredictability and its flexibility, given the freedom of a hospitable environment; but in the absence of that—Moon Dog's members, after all, live in a place where they do not or cannot work very often—the band simply created its own environment, devising its music at home in Oklahoma and carrying it elsewhere for public consumption. By 1981 the group had recorded two albums, experimenting in the studio without a producer to dictate what should be played or how to play it, and hoping to make its way without consorting with major record companies—and here one is reminded of Barney Kessel's preferences. As for its music, Moon

Dog could and did perform bluegrass, country and western, rhythm and blues, and rock, prompting Moore to remark that the group's principal influences were Earl Scruggs, Frank Zappa, and Slim Whitman. Their numbers were original compositions, with a smattering of pop favorites to catch audience attention, a customary ploy among bands with largely original repertoires. (As Terry Ware said one evening after he had brought down an Oklahoma City house with his joyous rendition of "Honky Tonk Man," Howard Hausey's hit of the 1950s for Johnny Horton, "Yessir, that's a real crowd pleaser.") Montgomery, a fine soloist, could blend his saxophone with any style, and Gill's amplified banjo could be made to sound like any of several instruments. Incongruous it may have seemed, but nothing succeeds like success.

In 1981 the band changed its name. The musicians had learned that somebody else had been using the name "for a long time," and no group that works fifty weeks a year wishes to become embroiled in litigation. The "somebody else" was, of course, none other than Louis Thomas Hardin, a New York street musician from Kansas by way of Wyoming, a performer on homemade instruments who became a cult figure in East Coast jazz circles in the 1940s and 1950s and whose stage name was Moondog. In the late 1950s, Hardin sued disc jockey Alan Freed over the use of the Moondog name, and Hardin won. So the band took the title of its first album, *Okiextremists*, and added it to what already was, becoming Okiextremists Moon Dog in time for the release of the second album. The group with the unlikely instrumentation now had an unlikely name as well; but the musicians perhaps knew that a name would not matter, not in Oklahoma. It would be another advertisement for the culture of the state, of course, but one that would be displayed in Canada or somewhere else.

There was little in Oklahoma in the early 1980s to indicate

that the state had ever played a major role—indeed, any role at all—in the development of jazz music. The Depression, in addition to everything else it did, appears to have been a cultural firebreak with regard to the growth of jazz in Oklahoma, the flames of innovation and improvisation dying behind it, cut off from the fuel of a vigorous cultural environment. Few clubs catered to a jazz-oriented clientele; and while a place like Bianca's in Oklahoma City might host a packed homecoming event for a native son like Barney Kessel, there was not a general perception that jazz even had a place in Oklahoma. In fact, many public officials seemed either to be ignorant of, or to ignore, the history of the Blue Devils, Jimmy Rushing, Charlie Christian, and all the rest; and when urban renewal threatened to raze those sections of Oklahoma City's Deep Second where so much of American jazz had its beginning, one spokesman decried efforts to preserve the dilapidated 1920s locales on the grounds that nothing important had happened there. That was the sort of mandatory statement required of anyone employed in urban renewal—destruction in the name of creation was prevalent in Oklahoma City in the 1970s as one quaint building after another fell to the demolition experts' dynamite in slow motion on the evening news—but it reflects also the level of cultural awareness prevalent in post-Depression Oklahoma: nothing important happened there. New Orleans, perhaps, or possibly New York, but not Oklahoma City. And nobody had read Ralph Ellison.

The principal event in Oklahoma jazz in 1980 was the issuance of a record album by state prison inmates. Entitled *Ain't Got Time to Lose,* the album of original compositions was prepared under the auspices of Institution Programs of Bartlesville, a nonprofit group developing prison arts programs, and followed a series of workshops conducted in the various prison facilities by Paul Brewer. On the basis of the recording, one could conclude that more jazz was being performed behind bars than was being played in them, in a state that once could boast of having some of the best jazz musicians in the nation.

The world of contemporary popular music in Oklahoma is a world underground. Each musician you meet will pass you along to another one, as if you were a refugee from a Top-Forty radio station in search of the obscure history of what amounts to a folk culture, as if you were a victim of electronic homogenization on the run to a promised land of musical ideas, of innovation, of cultural growth. It is a world that few who are not musicians will ever know—certainly not the adolescents who crowd the record stores on Saturday afternoon to purchase the vinyl of the latest rage; not the motoring citizens with radios tuned to stations that shape popular taste with preselected play-lists, or with tape decks handy beneath the dash for spice that propriety excludes from the ether; not the self-styled critics writing for college newspapers or the rock-oriented giveaway tabloids that make a fetish of pandering to superstars and ignoring their own environment; and not the elitists who call for an end to regionalism and would eradicate its last vestiges in favor of cosmopolitan culture, even in the face of history. No, that world is underground, where it thrives against all odds, and where the musicians pass you along from one to another as if you were a refugee.

In June, 1981, when I was attempting to finish this project (and coping with the certain knowledge that it would never be complete), I spoke again with Jim Herbst. He had more names, more underground stops for me to make. There was Phil Sampson, a Lawton songwriter who had provided T. G. Sheppard's current hit, "I Loved 'Em Every One." There was John Hadley, a composer and an artist and a poet whom I knew to be my colleague at the University of Oklahoma (though, at opposite ends of a large campus, we had never met), who had written

172

scores of songs, made an annual pilgrimage to Nashville to write and to study the music business, and who had once provided enough material for an entire album by singer Jim Stafford. And there was Alan Munde. I knew the name: Munde (pronounced Monday), a banjo player who had done some work with the public schools.

"He is one of the premier authorities on the banjo," Herbst said. "He is as good on the instrument as you can get. In the field of bluegrass music, the guy's a god."

I asked how I could get in touch with him. Herbst had a number. "Yes," he said, "he'll be expecting your call."

I was being passed along again.

Alan Munde was born in Norman in 1946. As a high school student in the heyday of the folk-music revival, he began studying guitar with Mike Richey, a jazz player who owned a Norman music store. Later, as Slim Richey of Richey Records in Fort Worth, he would produce Munde's albums for his Ridge Runner label, appearing occasionally in the liner credits as sideman for his former pupil. Munde stayed with the guitar for perhaps a year, then tried the banjo and found it more to his liking. He bought his first good banjo in 1964 and so confirmed his decision to take his music seriously.

Munde attended the University of Oklahoma and received a degree in education in 1969. In that year he turned professional and left for Nashville to perform with Jimmy Martin. Later, he moved to California and in 1972 joined a Los Angeles-based bluegrass group named Country Gazette. He has been with the group ever since.

Musically, what Alan Munde does on the banjo is evocative of what Barney Kessel does on guitar. There are improvisations and rearrangements of traditional material, and some of his playing has a definite jazzlike flavor. He has a major reputation and a national following, and, for those who care about such

173

things, he is John Hartford's favorite banjo player. But, like so many others, he cannot make a living in Oklahoma; he is on the road for six months out of the year, spending most of his time in the East, in performances from North Carolina to New York and occasionally to Boston. "In Oklahoma," he said, "you have to play what people hear on the radio." Outside the state reside the audiences for his music.

And yet, Munde still lives in Oklahoma. Despite the time and expense involved in travel to and from playing dates, he does not intend to move. Oklahoma is a nice place to live, he said, comfortable and familiar. "I like the look of the land. I like the people." He has performed in Oklahoma, but most recently in the public schools as part of an arts program, playing his music for classrooms of youngsters, many of whom had never seen a live performance (so pervasive is the influence of the broadcast media) and who seemed awed that another person standing in the same room with them could produce those sounds. Munde has done that sort of work because of his belief that personal music-making is important; and thus he is a living bridge between the vibrant cultural environment of Oklahoma's past and the young people who are the custodians of its cultural future. Though they have not known a time in their lives when music could not be had by turning a knob or flipping a switch, they are reminded of days when you made your own music if you were to have it at all; and they know that there are still Oklahomans who believe such activity essential for the well-being of the human soul. The lesson is that culture is alive and that it belongs to people.

I had too little time, and not enough of it to follow the underground connections to wherever they might lead. Munde, too, had names to offer. Terry Ware reminded me of Lyle Gaston, formerly a Woodward disc jockey, who had written a facetious country song in the 1950s entitled "Blackboard of My Heart," though I preferred the other side, "Salt of the Earth," about the good people one was likely to meet in northwestern Oklahoma. From the radio came the sound of David Frizzell and Shelly West singing "You're the Reason God Made Oklahoma," and the man at the microphone said that Larry Collins had written the words. Was this the Larry of Larry and Lorrie, the rockabilly Collins Kids of the 1950s? There was too little time and there were too few pages—all because there was so much music, so much of what I had once in a lecture described as "the Oklahoma history nobody knows."

Alan Munde recalled a story. Once, in an assembly at Norman High School, he had not stood up for the playing of "Oklahoma!" One of his teachers had seen him, and later, in class, the teacher had made something of a speech about the state song and how it deserved all the respect accorded to the national anthem. "I don't know why I didn't stand up," Munde told me. "It just seemed that the song didn't have anything to do with me."

Well, Woody Guthrie would not have stood either.

Sources

The textbook writer's comment may be found in Dan Williams, "Are They Doctoring Oklahoma History?" *Oklahoma Monthly,* March 1981, pp. 36-41. Donald Worster, *Dust Bowl: The Southern Plains in the 1930s* (New York: Oxford University Press, 1979) is the best introduction and may be supplemented by Paul Bonnifield, *The Dust Bowl: Men, Dirt, and Depression* (Albuquerque: University of New Mexico Press, 1979) and Walter J. Stein, *California and the Dust Bowl Migration* (Westport, Conn.: Greenwood Press, 1973). Michael Fessier, Jr., "From Dust They Did Return," *Oklahoma Monthly,* August 1977, pp. 23-31, and Bob Gregory, "From Dust They Did Return—Part 2," *Oklahoma Monthly,* September 1977, pp. 19-25, 124-29, are useful as well. Lingering concerns over *The Grapes of Wrath* are discussed in Bob Gregory, "Steinbeck's Legacy," *Oklahoma Monthly,* August 1976, pp. 56-63. The regents' meeting and its consequences are the subject of George Lynn Cross, *Presidents Can't Punt: The OU Football Tradition* (Norman: University of Oklahoma Press, 1977). See also the sources cited for chapter 10.

Terry Ware, Jim Herbst, and Dennis Meehan appear on Ray Wylie Hubbard, *Off the Wall* (Lone Star L-4603), which contains Hubbard's version of his "Redneck Mother." They are joined by Bill Shelton and Sid Aupperle (an Oklahoma City guitarist who occasionally performed with The Sensational Shoes) on Steve Weichert, *Oklahoma Bossa Nova* (Desire DSR-1), an album engineered by Herbst at No Sweat Studios, the joint venture of Meehan and Herbst. Meehan produced and engineered *The Clovis Roblaine Story* (No Sweat 00279), for which he composed all the music and on which he sang and played guitar, bass, keyboards, and drums; Meehan was, of course, Clovis Roblaine, a stage name he used even as an engineer/producer, and he was joined on the record by, among others, Ware, Herbst, Weichert, Dan Duggin, now a Woodward optometrist, and Jim Hochanadel, a versatile performer on saxophone, steel guitar, piano, harmonica, and several other instruments. Hochanadel, who has since performed with Jim Messina, appeared also on *The Lienke Brothers City Band* (No Sweat 00179) with Oklahoma City musicians Roger, Tom, and Tupper Lienke and Michael Dennis, an album that is another Roblaine effort. Herbst engineered, coproduced, and sided on Xebec, *Calm Before the Storm* (Desire DRS-3); that Oklahoma City band consisted of Jeff Parker, Kim May, Carl Goff, Jr., Mike Higgins, and Jeff Myers. Peter Polsgrove and Joe Montgomery, *Be Kind to Animals . . . And Feed Them Too* (Blue Moose BM 8001) is another No Sweat Studios product engineered by Roblaine, with Herbst, Roblaine, and pianist Morris Nelms included as sidemen. The Norman studio also produced several singles, including The Fensics, "Full Time Job/Tornado Warning" (No Sweat NSS-001), a 1979 release by a central Oklahoma punk-rock band that left for New York at the end of the following year. Terry Ware's solo album, *Caffeine Dreams* (Desire DSR-2), representing the last session work completed at No Sweat Studios, featured Shelton, Marlin Butcher, Herbst, Roblaine, and a number of other local musicians as sidemen.

Okiextremists Moon Dog, *Creatures of the Mind* (Root Records RR-1005), was engineered by Richard Bug for Oklahoma City's Unique Studio. This album and Ware's *Caffeine Dreams* both contain songs damning the club trend toward disco.

Alan Munde, *The Banjo Kid Picks Again* (Ridge Runner RRR-0022) is a release of 1980. A four-album Munde collection entitled *Festival Favorites*, a potpourri of bluegrass standards, begins with Volume 1 (Ridge Runner 0026).

Lyle Gaston, "Salt of the Earth/Blackboard of My Heart" (Hoss H-45-101), David Frizzell and Shelly West, "You're the Reason God Made Oklahoma" (Warner Bros. WBS 49650), and T. G. Sheppard, "I Loved 'Em Every One" (Warner Bros. WBS 49690) are relevant to the discussion.

The years by themselves do not make a place historic. It is men who give the color of history to a place by their deeds there or by merely having lived there.

— Simeon Strunsky

Nothing that was worthy in the past departs; no truth or goodness realized by man ever dies, or can die; but is all still here, and, recognized or not, lives and works through endless changes.

— Thomas Carlyle

Index

182

Index

Twilley, Dwight: 130

University of Chicago, Chicago, Ill.: 129
University of Oklahoma, Norman, Okla.: 67, 135, 156, 165, 172, 173
University of Texas, Austin, Texas: 83

Vian, Okla.: 148
Von Ronk, Dave: 13

Wagoner, Okla.: 115
Wakely, Jimmy: 39, 41, 43, 148
Walker, Jim Daddy: 50
Walker, Wayne P.: 149-50
Wand, Hart: 11, 12
Wapanucka, Okla.: 112
Ware, John: 123
Ware, Terry: 165-68, 170, 174
WBAP radio: 145
Webb, Jimmy: 153-54
Webster, Ben: 27
Weichert, Steve: 165, 166, 167
Wellston, Okla.: 77
Wess, Frank: 28
Whitley, Ray: 39, 41-43
Wiley, Lee: 102-103

Williams, Claude: 16, 94
Williams, John B.: 33
Willis, Guy: 82, 88
Willis, Skeeter: 82, 88
Willis, ("Uncle") Wallis: 5, 155
Willis, Vic: 82, 83, 88
Wills, Bob: 13-14, 15, 36, 38, 43, 57, 58, 86, 155, 161-62; repertoire of, 16
Wilson, Charlie: 131
Wilson, Jimmy: 39
Wilson, Robert: 131
Wilson, Ronnie: 131
Winslett, Millidge: 21
WKY radio: 41
WLS radio: 39
Woodward, Okla.: 165, 167, 174
Wooley, Sheb: 145-47
Worster, Don: 161
Wright, Dan: 113
Wrightsman, Stan: 104
WSM radio: 149

Xavier University of Louisiana, New Orleans, La.: 108
Xebec: 166, 176

Young, Lester: 23, 27, 28, 90, 91, 97
Youngblood, Harry: 22

185

Singing Cowboys and All That Jazz,

designed by Sandy See and Edward Shaw, was set by the University of Oklahoma Press in 10½-point Souvenir, a contemporary typeface selected to harmonize with the subject, and was printed offset on 60-pound Warren's #66 Antique, a permanized sheet, with presswork by the University of Oklahoma Printing Services and binding by the Becktold Company.